The Healer Within

The Healer Within

*My journey to healing myself
while healing others through my gift
as a psychic clairvoyant*

ELLEN MORRIS

Providing professional book design, editing and printing services
for indie authors to tell their stories

accentia.com.au

First published 2021

Copyright © Ellen Morris, 2021
Revised 28 June 2021

The moral right of the author has been asserted.

All rights reserved. Without limiting the rights under copyright restricted above, no part of this publication may be reproduced, in any form or by any means (electronic, mechanical, photocopying, recording or otherwise), without the prior written permission of both the copyright owner and the publishing partner of this book.

Cover Design, Typesetting, Editing: Accentia Design
Typeset in 14/16 pt Garamond & Friz Quadrata
Self Publishing Partner: Accentia Design Pty Ltd for Ellen Morris
Cover illustration: © 2020 by Carmen Mountford

Printed in Australia

The publishing partner, staff, agents and authors are not liable for injuries or damage occasioned to any person as a result of reading or following the information contained in this book. The views and recollections expressed in this book are the authors own. People named within the book have agreed and given permission for their stories and names to be published.

A Cataloguing-in-Publication record is available from the National Library of Australia. http://catalogue.nla.gov.au

ISBN: **978-0-6451561-0-2** (Paperback)

To Cathy

You will walk and work with me till we meet again big Sis. Through losing you I found a place I never dreamed I could be—devoting my life to heal others and for those who live your pain daily in this lifetime.

In doing so I found my own strength and healed, while showing others how to escape the dark rabbit hole and to find the magic one with their own unique key to freedom which they had all along.

Fly free big Sis.
My love for you goes unspoken.

"I learnt to never mix my spirits with Spirits..."

– *Ellen Morris*

Ellen Morris

*Psychic Clairvoyant, Holistic Healer,
Reiki Master & Motivational Speaker,
Author*

CONTENTS

Prologue	i
My Magic Rabbit Hole	1
Moving on and on...	5
Never let the Magic Die	9
Wrighty	13
Love at First Sight	19
Unforgettable Cathy	29
The Unthinkable	39
My Rollercoaster ride down into the Dark Rabbit Hole	43
Grammy Time	47
Down the Magic Rabbit Hole	53
Finding my Red Shoes	61
Finding the Gift of Reiki	67
Shazell Comes to Life	73
My World Changes	79
The World is put on Hold—Covid-19	81
Covid Slows while the World Hurts	89
Back to my Magic Carpet Ride	91
Never a dull Moment	95
The Bay Getaway	99
Dean makes his Entrance	103
Stepping up to the Stage	109
Pocket Rocket	115
Crazy Covid	121
Meeting Amanda Jane	125
Dedication to our beautiful Clair	129
Finding your Key to Happiness	135
Set Yourself Free	141
Rebirth at the Waterfalls	147
In their own Words	154
I . am . Me	163

Prologue

Well, here I am at last—in print!

Many years ago, a psychic told me, 'Ellen you will write a book'—I had a little laugh to myself as I can't spell the best. My mind boggled as to what it—the book—would be about.

The life of a psychic clairvoyant is not an easy one. It seems we aren't accepted by many. I understand this because what we can't see in life we tend not to believe—yet to the clairvoyant — it is our world.

Through a lot of heartache in my life from a very young age, I learned to escape the pain of the world and instead immerse myself in my own world of magic—a world full of joy, a world full of love that no one could destroy.

So what if I told you I could give you a key to your own freedom and happiness? better still... what if I showed you that you've had that key in your pocket all along?

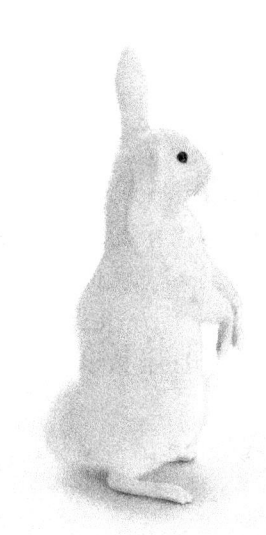

CHAPTER 1

My Magic Rabbit Hole

Why am I writing a book on my life? I have written it in the hope that you can find your own key. If I only knew I had the key to freedom all along and believed in Ellen Louise—my life may have been quite different.

You see I never felt I fit in. All my life I felt so different to all those around me. As a child I thought everyone saw and felt spirit like me. When I would play and make up fun games everyone would come and play with me. I had a great imagination. I could bring magic to life.

I guess back then I always felt like a leader. As a child the imagination can take us to wherever we want to be. It can also take us away from the places we don't want to be – especially if we cannot face what has hurt us in our young lives.

I talk about my 'magic rabbit hole' throughout this book. For me my life has had many ups and downs. When I could not cope with what was happening in my life, I would escape into my magic place as a coping mechanism.

The innocent mind of a child learns to cope in many ways. I was running from the dark rabbit hole I could not face–to the magic one that was safe and comforting.

Little did I know, later in life I would see how this saved me and still does.

As a young child, the first time I used this magic was to escape the man in the mask—who I grew to know as the lolly man. When he would enter my room, I would hide under my bed. It was dark and I was alone and I would take myself to the magic rabbit hole where I felt safe.

I spoke of him many times in my life to so many people—yet sadly no one would listen to me as my story was not clear. Later in life I learnt the mind can block a trauma like this for many years and that we develop coping mechanisms.

I learnt about this when I started having clear flash backs of smells and surroundings of the events that had stolen my childhood. Being a clairvoyant doesn't always work in my favour — this was to be one of my hardest lessons.

You see I knew this person was real, but as a psychic, it was often seen as storytelling—so in the end I gave up and thought maybe it was something I had brought to life in my head. How sad to look back and see myself trying to get someone to listen to my story for all those years.

I was told by my psychiatrist up to eighty percent of us who have been through a trauma like this will block it out until and if we are strong enough. Many who come to see me at Shazell have been the same.

As time went on, I went to many healers and readers—every one of them asked me the same question... what happened to me as a child. One of them even clearly described an article of clothing he always wore.

Once the healing I was about to face started—during Covid-19 lockdown—there was no denying who this person was and what had taken place. This was again so hard as an active psychic. So many thought this was just what I had been told and came to believe.

I can understand why so many don't speak up, as they are put on trial for something they don't want to relive—myself included. So much so even I went into self doubt around what had happened. I'm so grateful now that I began believing in myself and did and do not care, who believes me. The most important part is that I believe in me at last! Why would I have spent so many years looking for approval and acknowledgement through these people. Those who know me, know I would not write a book or share this story unless I knew it was true.

As you read on you will see how owning my key is owning my freedom.

I own who I am and who I was—and this book is my final way of setting myself free.

~~~~~

To have my gift is a blessing I love, yet again many don't believe this part of me either. I understand—what we cannot see we tend to not believe at times. Let's face it—there are a lot of fakes out there and this makes me sad as I know many who are so gifted and use this gift to only share love and healing—just as I do.

Those who know me would know my life work is my heart and soul work. My only regret is I listened to those who judged and laughed at me for way too long—and wasted this precious gift.

So, if you are reading this now with doubt—I get you. I had my own doubts for many years. The things I have delivered from the other side over the past six years has showed me I should have accepted this blessing and accepted Ellen Louise for all that she is.

My book is raw—I share so much of my roller-coaster ride I call my life with you.

Why did I write this? Simple... if one thing in this book saves someone from a dark rabbit hole—my job is done.

I hope you enjoy my story and you take something from it and find your own magical key.

Bless be.
    Ellen xx

CHAPTER 2

Moving on and on...

About three years after Daddy—or Daddy G as I call him—had passed, Mum fell in love with the man who would become our stepfather—and adopt my sister Cathy and I as his own. He worked in a bank at Maitland at the time. He soon got another job as a broker at Wagga Wagga, so we moved out of the only place I could remember as home.

I missed my grandparents so much—Maitland felt so far away living in cold old Wagga Wagga.

My best memories in life were school holidays. My grandparents owned a beautiful big old house at Corlette and we would pack up and go there every holiday. Sometimes it would just be Cathy and me, and at Christmas time it was something special. It would be the whole family and all my cousins, aunts and uncles. My beautiful Nanna (who was my great grandmother) lived in a flat to the side of my grandparents house. The first thing you could smell when we arrived after the long drive, was her amazing cooking. She was like Mother Mary to me, such a saint.

Nanna had a pet spider called Harry—he was huge! all the other kids were scared of him, but not me. I loved when he was watching over me. They also had a real grandma's feather bed that we all loved to go and jump on as soon as we got there.

We would run along the beach day and night, swim and go out in the little tinnie they bought us. I loved to go out in the big boat with the men to fish—I guess I always loved the fresh air and being outside and I was a bit of a tomboy.

∾∾ ∾∾ ∾∾

The most special time was the big Christmas party up at the park. Santa would come in on a boat and sit on the back of a big truck and hand out toys. I would nearly burst when he called my name—the whole magic of him coming and bringing these things from the North Pole. The pictures in my imagination of all the elves and helpers was the world I loved.

At one of the party's I remember sitting there so excited waiting for my name to be called so I could climb up on that truck and tell Santa how happy I was he shared his joy all over the world... and also how clever his magic was. Cathy burst my bubble big time by saying "that's not Santa... he's not real". She said "watch when I go up... I'll pull his beard off. It's Grandfather and it's him Christmas day... why do you think he's never there Christmas morning?". I saw a face I knew and loved. Instead of getting upset I ran around thinking my grandfather was Santa. This was why he went to bed before us Christmas eve.

∾∾ ∾∾ ∾∾

Not long after this Mum sat me down and told me, "Ellen, Santa is grandfather, he is not real, neither is the tooth fairy or all your friends you talk to that we cannot see." My heart sank. "No Mummy, Grandfather may not be Santa, but fairies and my friends are real."

That night I went under my bed and down my magic rabbit hole. I talked to all my friends and decided I'll never turn the magic off as then I would have no safe place to go–and most of all I knew it was real. I felt confused that day—I didn't understand why others didn't see what I saw.

CHAPTER 3

Never let the Magic Die

My lesson here was never let the magic die. Why do you think fairy tales were made? They are the best tools ever. They teach us good and bad, and the good always wins in the end.

The song 'Don't Stop Believing' goes through my head as I sit here now.

Our biggest lessons in life happen at a young age. If we teach our children to wish upon a star and that dreams can come true, it can, and if we teach them evil is bad energy, we can learn to try to avoid it. We are all simply energy... are we not? So, if kids are taught to feel safe in good energy and move away from bad energy, then we are winning.

So why did child Ellen go down the rabbit hole? because she felt safe.

Would she run out the back and walk off with the man in the mask? No, because that was an energy she felt sick and scared of. Though to make it simple. She would always know with her instinct what felt good and what felt bad.

I lived so happily in my world of magic; I still do. I will never let anyone take that away from me. Really what would I do without my fairy spies and many guides I met along the way.
In Wagga Wagga there was lots of magic to be found.

A younger sister was born, and I could see so many magic things around her and her toys as she grew. It's also the place where Cathy first started showing signs of her mental illness.

We would be walking to school (crazy now to think that back in the day it was safe enough to walk) in a group of friends at such a young age to school and Cathy would say "I cannot Ellen, please go to school with our friends."

I would never leave her there alone—even to the last day of her life she knew I was here. I would look down and she would be in the gutter making herself sick. Day after day, week after week we would go through the same thing. I would try and teach her my magic and give her my strength, but I just could not make her be like me. It made me sad.

I would invite her into my magic world to play in trees and make up the best games. I would get excited when she would talk to all my spirit friends. I wish she could have seen the magic through my eyes and how I used it to get me through so many dark times in my life. Looking back I know they were past souls. I wanted to share the magic in my world and teach her how to take away her pain but that never happened.

Wagga Wagga was such a cold place. I remember we would wake up to frost covering the ground like snow. Dad went mad because he couldn't get the ice off the car to go to work, while Mum would be laughing because the toilet was frozen.

I love the cold, always have, so when we would go next door some mornings to have breakfast with our friends—while Mum tended to the baby—I would be in my warm bubble. They always had the fire going and we would cook our crumpets that Mum would send with us, toasting them over the fire. Then we would start groundhog day... trying to get Cathy to school.

With all the magic around me I guess I used it as a tool to try to heal her.

∽∽ ∽∽ ∽∽

I got home one afternoon, and the big wooden boxes were out. This meant we were moving again.

Dad had been transferred to Tamworth.

I was so sad to leave all my friends, but my life journey had another place ahead for me and so we packed and headed off on our yellow brick road to yet another place to live.

We settled quickly and started at a new school. This meant high anxiety for Cathy again. So, the long, morning journey to school started again. She had her days and I always watched over her from afar. Cathy excelled at school, so when she settled and focused, her report cards were always full of A+ and nothing but high praise.

∽∽ ∽∽ ∽∽

One afternoon after school Mum told us the good news... she was having another baby! I screamed with joy. So, nine months latter my first brother was born. Life just seemed to flow on, and my magic kept me safe and happy. There were so many special places I found to play there - a tree could be a whole world of magic to me.

Just as I began to feel happy and settled, I came home to the packaging boxes again lined up down the hallway. Oh no.

This turned out to be our last childhood move, and it was a great one.

CHAPTER 4

Wrighty

We settled in quickly and started school at Floraville in NSW. This was a huge part of my life with so many life lessons. Cathy also settled in quickly and came into her own. We would catch the bus to school, and she would skip along ahead. I seemed to find my voice here and was forever in trouble for talking.

I was sat with the quietest person in the classroom - Sharon and our beautiful magical friendship began. I bit my fingernails with the nerves I was starting to feel, and her first words seeing me do this were "do you have a rabbit habit?".

How funny she said this to me at the time, and especially now when reflecting back to where it all began. Here I am now teaching people how to escape their rabbit hole.

To be honest I thought she was a bit of a dag at first. As soon as she said she was getting a cement pond—as she called it our friendship was set in concrete. I also learnt very quickly that Sharon was such a sweet person. She was brought up with rules and she stuck by them. That quickly changed under my wayward influence, yet we remained friends for many years. Our parents became great friends as well. Life was great.

Mum came home one day and told me she had been to the doctors and that "she had killed the rabbit". I was so upset as she told me "if you're pregnant, the rabbit dies". I've always been very gullible to say the least. So, it ends up she was simply trying to telling me she was having another baby not killing rabbits. Phew! When my brother was born Shaz fell in love with him. I would say "let's go for a walk" and out she would come with him in a pram.

She spent so much time with him and I could see why. Later on in life she started working with special needs children. Shaz was a natural and with her beautiful heart and nature, it was the perfect fit for her gentle ways.

One night we stayed at her place and set up a séance. We were up under the house and found this old Ouija board. I must admit I was pushing away to scare her—next thing it took off under my finger like crazy. Wow! Spirit showed me a few things that night! Shaz started screaming and moving her hands around in front of her face. "The old lady, the old lady" she said. We both went white with fright. We left the board under the house and ran upstairs. We sat in her room asking each other if we were acting. She swore she wasn't; I know I wasn't. The lesson here—don't mess with the unknown until you learn more and be careful what you wish for.

We went through high school and stuck like glue as best friends for life. We got asked to a party next door to hers place one night, where at the young age of fifteen I met Greg (who would turn out to be the love of my life).

Life changed to one big party. One night her parents said they were going to Sydney the next day to stay the night. We saw this as an opportunity to have fun. Word got out big time - thanks to me - that we were having a pool party. Oh dear... was that a big one! and it got out of hand so quick. The beautiful wrought iron table setting ended up in the pool. All the bottles of antique wine got drunk, then I turned to see something go through her mums' pride and joy—her fish tank. I ran and grabbed a container, got water and was grabbing the fishies and throwing them into the Esky as quickly as I could to try to save them. As I looked around there were about six people jumping on her mums' bed—then boom! crash!... it broke as well. Someone had gone out and opened the bird aviary and the birds were flying away. Oh shit... we are dead, I thought.

Next thing I heard yelling. I went out and what I saw was not good. Shaz's Mum and partner had come home—and someone was patting her Mums' partner on his shiny bald head saying "cheer up old mate, have a beer."

That was it —I was told to get out and never come back.

Shaz was not allowed to ring me or I her. I rushed around school looking for her on the Monday. I couldn't find her anywhere and thought she must be having the day off. When I got home I found out she had been sent to Sydney to a private girl's school. I was devastated.

∽∽ ∽∽ ∽∽

It took a long time but finally Shaz could come stay during school holidays—I was so happy to see her. We learned a big lesson that night. True friendship cannot be broken. She moved home again, and we finished school. She got a job at Flemings Supermarket with me. We worked all week and partied and layed around the beach all weekend.

It was the perfect teenagers life.

Shaz met a few guys and went out with them. I was madly in

love with Greg but always had time for Shaz. She settled down with Greg's best mate and informed me she would be marrying him in our back yard. Me being me—I couldn't say no—even when I was six weeks out from having my third baby. We both had three beautiful children and spent every special occasion with them, as one big family.

I remember the day Shaz came down to tell us they were moving to Queensland. My heart sank—she was being taken away from me again—it was a very teary farewell. They would come and visit, as we would them, but I'd lost my little mate.

Little did I know that, that farewell would be nothing on the news that was to come.

∾∾ ∾∾ ∾∾

It was Christmas day and my perfect little world was rocked to its foundations when I found out—Shaz had cancer.

She was so sick the last time I saw her. This tiny little thing walked up and said "Hello McInerny" (we called each other Wrighty and McInerney). If Steven wasn't with her, I wouldn't have known it was her. I felt my feet going from under me, my world was spinning and I bravely held back my tears. We were staying across the road from the hospital and we left after a long visit. I could see it was wearing her out and we needed to go and rest after the long drive up to visit her. I thought I was about to pass out in the car park with the shock and pain that weighed heavily in my chest and heart.

Steven was taking us out for tea—I couldn't go, I was a mess—I have always been tough and worn my mask well, but not now.

We stayed the weekend and it was one of the hardest things I ever had to do. Putting my mask back on and acting brave for her, we went to say what would be our final goodbyes ever. She looked in my eyes and said 'I'll beat this and see you at Easter, okay?', I hugged her tiny body and said "yes". I knew I would never see her in this life again.

On the first day of spring as the sun came up, she closed her eyes and crossed the bridge. She was and will always be the sunshine in my day. My best little mate left me way too soon. My heart was broken.

We went up for her funeral. I walked in and the only thing on her coffin was my purple bear with a necklace I gave her, placed gently upon it.

Prior to the funeral, there was a psychic site on Facebook I had been drawn to. One of the readers and I started to talk a lot. She helped me through to the day of her funeral and told me I would speak at her funeral. "No way!" I said—she was good at her job—and so it was, I got up and spoke.

I don't know how but I somehow managed to stand there and through the tears, spoke about my beautiful Shaz. I guess it was the first time she showed me how to be on stage with her right beside me in spirit.

We talked that night as I lay sobbing holding the bear the family had passed on to me. Shaz had told them to make sure I got him.

∽∽ ∽∽ ∽∽

I got home and about a month later and I could no longer find the psychic woman's details that I'd met at the Fair... funny how spirit works–her job was done, and so she was gone.

I wish I could find her and bless her with a return reading for all her support. Funny this was her name was Sherrie; the same pet name Sharon's dad had called her too.

This was not the end for me and my little mate Shaz, she still works with me every day when doing readings and teaching... she's always around me.

CHAPTER 5

Love at First Sight

In most fairy tales there is a prince and a princess. I found my prince at the tender age of just fifteen. The irony of it, is funny now I look back. He walked into to a party next door to Sharon's. I said to my friend, "who is that?", they replied "that's Pixie".

How fitting... as most who know me in Shazell call me *Fairy El*. I do believe there was some divine intervention going on here.

Greg came and sat with me—and I'll never forget our first conversation—so ironic again. It was about cremation of all things. Many girls would have left there and then yet I sat there completely captivated by his wisdom. It did end with me having the last say—as it still does lol—I was so drawn to him.

The night was coming to an end and I was gone—hook line and sinker—he caught my heart that night. Greg asked if he could walk me home and I laughed and said, "yes, although I'm only staying next door". He said "well we may have to take the long way home".

So, as we hit the laneway, I noticed Shaz following us— if looks could kill. Next thing I felt an arm go around me... it was another guy I had been chatting with who thought I'd given him the signal I was interested. So, Greg ended up walking with Shaz as I was too shy to tell the other guy I wasn't interested and that I wanted to walk with Greg.

We got home and I said to Shaz "if you kissed him your dead!". To this day I still don't know if she did or not.

I could not wait to see Greg again. At the next party we spent the whole night chatting, laughing and sealed the night with a passionate kiss. We were so young and free and we spent all our time at the beach and partying. The simplicity of our teenage years.

One night we turned up to a party and Greg forgot to get smokes, so we took off up the channel at Swansea to get some for the night. What happened next was a bit of a blur... all I know was that I was stuck in the car we'd been driving that was being held up by a pole in the bloody Swansea channel! Everyone jumped out yet they didn't realise I was still stuck in the car. I thank all my angels they got me out as the water was rising inside the car—apart from being black and blue from head to toe for a while—I was fine, as was everyone in the car. Unfortunately the car wasn't so looking so flash. Greg's dad wouldn't be impressed.

Greg's dad loved a good bargain and brought so many cars—as I was to learn over the years—and this car was a new one... and it was a total write-off. The accelerator had stuck, we hit a bend going too fast and there was no getting out of what happened next.

I had not met Greg's dad at this stage— he was a seaman and away a lot—so, my first time meeting him was just a tad uncomfortable. Greg has a huge family—so it took a while to meet them all and they grew to be part of my world and I love them all.

It didn't take me long to say the 'L' word, and I was over the moon when he said "I love you too... will you be my girl?". I spent every day I could, staying at his house. I remember going there one night and all the family were smiling and looking at my finger. I was thinking 'wow this is strange'... then Greg took me into his room and gave me the most beautiful ring! I was bursting with happiness.

My fairy tale was coming to life.

∞ ∞ ∞

We moved into a sweet little apartment right on the beach at Caves Beach. Life was magic, my peace, love and mung bean days as I call it. I had a job as a seamstress at Wall Jones and Greg was landscaping. We were so in love and so happy. I thought life couldn't get any better.

Well, it did... you see the missing part of my fairytale was to become a mother. We had a little chat and I said "I think I need a break off the pill". Greg said "okay". I quickly asked "what if I fall pregnant?", he said, "we have a baby". Always matter of fact and to the point my Greg.

It was only a few weeks later I was so sick of a morning every day at work. I would perk up at lunch time and by tea time, cooking would make me so sick I couldn't eat a thing... now not eating is definitely not me. I think if a hot chicken went passed my coffin my hand would go out and grab that last feed!

It didn't even enter my mind I could be pregnant this quick. I went to the doctors and told him my signs and he smiled and said, "do you think you could be pregnant Ellen?" The doctor did a blood test and told me to come back in five days. That Friday I went back with a friend for my results. I'd told Greg I would meet him for drinks when he finished work. That was not quite how it played out.

I went into my appointment and the words "Congratulations

Mummy!" rolled out of the doctor's mouth as I walked into his office. Okay... whoops! I'll never forget sitting there and being completely blown away by his words.

∽∽ ∽∽ ∽∽

I was born to be a mother, yet there's no denying it... the shock was massive. I knew within minutes and I was over the moon. I walked out and my friend was sitting waiting for me to tell her the results. I couldn't tell her – Greg needed to know first. I guess my ashen grey face with eyes as huge as dinner plates and the fact I could not talk, gave it away.

Of all places to find out—I went home and Greg had already gone over to the pub. No mobiles in those day to say 'come home I need to talk to you'. So big breaths and into the pub I walked — he was at the bar. I called him over and he yelled out "do you want a beer?". Shaking my head, he looks at me strangely and I could see the look of confusion on his face and what he was thinking... 'what?, she doesn't want a drink?... it's Friday'.

So, he comes over and we walk out for some privacy and I tell him—I don't think I took a breath for a while—he grabbed me, so happy and went in to tell his mates and shout the bar. So different in our day as we hadn't even told our parents yet.

The next day I was so worried as we drove to tell Mum and my step-father. I was scared of his temper. To my shock, Mum jumped up so happy— I'll never forget her face and she shed a tear. That was easy! so now I am getting really excited.

Next stop was to see Greg's Mum and Dad—they were also thrilled for us. The news spread quickly and everyone was so happy for us. We spoke of getting married—as it was the done thing back in the day. We decided not to get married at the time, as we knew our love was strong enough to not need a piece of paper and to spend a big chunk of money to prove our love for each other... we really needed the money for this little human we had created.

I absolutely loved being pregnant. You would see me coming in my crazy bright clothes and crazy hair. I nested well and could not wait to meet this little human made with love. He was spoiled by everyone as I was the first in our group to have a baby and our parents loved to make things for him.

The baby was due to arrive December 6th. After one false alarm and being told "go home-it was not time" as my labour stopped. My dream of becoming a Mum came true when he finally decided to enter my world on December 22nd... after a very long and natural drug free labour.

Joshua Adam was just perfect—a mass of black hair and the sweetest little face I had ever seen. It was love at first sight for the second time in my life. I will never forget the love I felt sitting on my bed looking at this perfect little human our love had made.

Counting his fingers and toes and kissing each one and smothering his face in butterfly kisses as tears rolled down my cheeks. My mother was standing in the hall watching this—full of pride and joy for me. He was a perfect baby and motherhood came so easy to me. Watching him grow and our love grow with him was pure magic.

We decided it was time to have another baby we could give all this love too. I said "I would like to be married first this time". So, we planned our wedding and our family catered for our special day.

You know that fairy-tale wedding every woman dreams of? Well, we started by picking April 13 to be our special day. The celebrant asked "are you not superstitious?". I said "no, why?", he said "well it's the only date available as no one wants it".

So, the big day I dreamed of all my life arrived.

We both loved the beach so we chose to be married at the Pilot Station at the top of Swansea Heads overlooking all our favourite beaches—the reception was held at Caves Beach Surf Club.

I woke that morning to the most amazing sunny day and thought 'how blessed am I'. Oh how things can turn in two hours—it was now flogging down with rain. Here we were at the hairdressers and Greg is still calling — the wedding is still going ahead at the Heads as planned.

I look back and laugh now but so much went wrong that day I could write another book on it! pardon the pun. In the end I married my prince to live happily ever after.

We were now all set to start trying to fall again. I fell the first month with Josh so I was so shocked every month when I found I hadn't fallen pregnant again. Then from day one, I just knew I had another little human growing inside of me.

I still think childbirth is the most amazing, magical thing ever.

I went to the doctor and couldn't believe it when my blood work came back negative. I didn't believe him, and just told everyone that I was pregnant and started planning ahead. I went back a month later for a follow up test and funnily enough, he said "yes... now you're pregnant." About time he caught up with what my body already knew.

Nine months from when I said I was pregnant from the first test, Aarron Graham came into the world—upside down. After a drug free perfect first birth, I didn't know what had hit me! He had turned and wrapped his cord around his neck so I had to hold him in till it was safe to deliver. Love at first sight for a third time. My first look at him, after all that hard work—he looked so much like Josh, I thought I was seeing double. Then I noticed his trademark birthmark on his tiny neck and his little chubby face—he was absolutely perfect in every way.

Those trademark cheeks earned him the name 'Chopper'. His love of football started at five with Greg coaching him and we all yelled "Go Chopper!". I have stood and given him the chop signs at a grand final where he was the captain and coach. Now many years later Aarron still lives for football and now coaches his own son.

If you asked me, what does he love more? KFC or football? ...I still couldn't tell you to this day.

Me and my boys—to me life was complete.

A few times Greg asked if I wanted to try for a girl. I would say "no, you boys are all I need".

It got me thinking that maybe I should give him his wish. One night I whispered to him "Okay... I know it will be a girl - now let's do this!"... I didn't have to ask him twice! Just like before, in the first month, my tiny dancer was conceived. I was so excited and went straight out and bought everything I could find that was pink.

All my friends kept saying 'what if it's not a girl?', my reply was "a mother just knows". By this time technology had come a long, long way, so I was so excited to book in for a scan to show them all—and I guess shut them all up—that I was in fact having a girl.

In true Cody style she had her legs crossed and no matter how hard we tried during the scan, she was not going to let us know. I didn't worry as I knew in my heart it was a girl. I created the most beautiful nursery - ready for my princess. Every first-born girl in every generation on Mum's side was a Scorpio and she keep the tradition going.

Cody Kay came into the world like a little mermaid —they were trying to tell me I wasn't in labour and they were taking me back to the ward. I grabbed the poor nurse by the arm and said "have you had a baby?", she said "no". I said "...well I've had two and very soon it will be three". They gave me a huge shot of pethidine—to shut me up, I still think to this day. Next thing my water broke and I don't even think I pushed; Cody literally flew out as the nurse threw her gloves on just in time to catch her.

That's my girl... never one to wait!

She wasn't breathing so they rushed her off in a humidicrib so quick—it all felt so different to the boy's births. When I walked up to look at her, again my heart was overflowing - it was love at first sight. She was so tiny and perfect. The boys had both been born with a mass of black hair. She had such a tiny face and all this light, wispy, angel-like hair.

She gave us a few scares that first week but I had my fairy princess and my family was complete. She's grown to be a beautiful you woman who is my best friend and my rock.

∽∽ ∽∽ ∽∽

My children are my world and I love them with every beat of my heart. How they love to hear my flat earth stories every time we celebrate Christmas. The look they give me when I do many of my 'Ellen-isms' as we call them, is priceless. They all have my back and I love them for that.

I love them for loving me with all my crazy mannerisms that make me who I am.

There were times in my life I would not have made it through without the love Greg and my children give me—so I know I'm truly blessed.

One by one they found love in their lives. Josh found his Princess Tanya – and fled the nest. Aarron found his Princess

Michelle—or he would never have fled the nest. Cody found her Prince Corey and even though many times in her life—as the hump on my back as we called her—she would say "I'll never find a prince and leave you...", but she did.

They all picked the best and the fact they're all happy is all part of the magic.

Love at first sight is the best magic in my life.

CHAPTER 6

Unforgettable Cathy

My big sister Cathy—where do I begin with you sweetheart? Once we moved to Newcastle there was no stopping you girl. We were only thirteen months apart in age—you felt more like my twin than my older big sis. You filled my world with so many different emotions. I'm sure you're my soul sister and I know we will meet up again one day. I hope you are with our Daddy G—I'm sure he was waiting for you at the other side of the rainbow bridge.

I know one thing... the whole time we were together all I ever said was "Cathy, don't do that!" - you were always up to so much mischief.

You became very popular at Floraville School and became School Captain. You were a boy magnet, and once in high school, met your first love.

I had never seen you so happy—finally I felt I could let you live without constantly watching over you.

High School treated you well—you pair were the love couple of Belmont High. Sadly, this was also the time your borderline personality disorder set in, and a need to be noticed took over.

You lost the love of your life to a silly mistake and you cried night and day for months. I don't think you ever really got over him—as the last week of your life you were speaking like you were back with him again.

Cathy was in a bad car accident at Nelsons Bay after she left school where she was thrown through the windscreen of the car. Cathy was also the biggest hypochondriac and loved hospital... but not this time. Her face was so badly injured that when I went to see her— I walked straight past her bed. I could hear my name being called but surely that couldn't be my beautiful sister? One of her friends came to visit, saw her, passed out, and ended up in the bed next to her.

When she finally came home again, she cried and cried.

I just wanted to fix my Big Sis.

I lay and cried myself to sleep many nights but never let her know this. I was the strong sister, she was the Big Sister. It's just the way we were.

∽∽ ∽∽ ∽∽

Oh boy, did her roller coaster go off the rails then? and where do I start?

So many memories, so funny and yet so sad at the same time. We just never knew what we would get day by day with you. Borderline personality disorder is so hard to control. Poor Cathy could be so up and wild, then so down and tucked away under the doona, embarrassed - for weeks at a time.

One night we were all sitting in the lounge room and down she came with a totally see-through dress on. No underpants needed as she had been to the beauty parlour she said. "Oh my!... Cathy, don't do that" I said. She came back with "You're such a prude, Ellen." She was on her way to her work Christmas party. So off she trotted in her see-through dress with not a care in the world. She came home saying how cold her, and the guy she picked up were in the Civic Fountain. The thing with her was you didn't laugh and forget it—you knew what she was saying was true. Funny thing was she didn't go back to work after the Christmas party.

∽∽ ∽∽ ∽∽

Then there was the time we were having a nice birthday party for my daughter when she was little, I looked up and thought 'why is everyone looking like that at my kitchen window. I got up to take a look and to my horror, I looked up to see Cathy boldly chucking a brown-eye at everyone... like it's a two-year old's party for hecks sake, Cathy!!

So, in I went, and the old "Cathy don't do that!" was yelled this time. There was no telling what she might be up to next.

∽∽ ∽∽ ∽∽

Cathy would cause so much trouble and made up songs that were hurtful. You would know as she would ring or walk in and say whoops... "Cathy what have you done?", then you would wait for the answer that would come from someone she'd upset.

She eventually found her drug of choice, and it would calm her to "normal", she would say. One night we had a party and that day we had received a delivery of the new tiles for the bathroom and laundry. Cathy had been missing for a while, so I went to check on her. Cathy had found the tiles and laid the whole bathroom to show us. That was so Cathy. She was great as she never sat still and cleaned up over and over all night long.

Later that night I heard a lot of noise inside, I came in to see she had done war paint (as Cathy liked to call it) all over her face and body with no top on (she had her breasts reduced and thought they were amazing). In true Cathy style she casually said 'who needs smokes I'm off to the shop?"... and off she went, boobs all decorated and face paint and got her smokes. Not a care in the world.

She had also convinced herself she had made a hole in the top of her mouth from a lot of self-medicating. I don't know how many times she made me look, bless her. It was all fun on the night but the day after that party she went under the doona for days as she had really upset a few people with her song making.

༺ ༺ ༺

Another great unforgettable Cathy moment was when I had not long had my son Aarron—my second blessing in life. I was at home and a few of them went out over the road to the golf club for drinks. Suddenly the door flung open and Cathy rolled in. She was screaming, "I've been hit by a truck and they left me there, I've been laying in the median strip for an hour and they all drove past and left me."

She carried on the story and the drinking for hours. We ran out of drink, so she snuck around to my Mum's, who lived in the same units as us after she finally left my step father. I had gone to bed and left them to play. The next morning my Mum was so upset to find a bottle of drink–that had survived the Maitland floods–was missing. Cathy had gone home to Mum's and emptied out the bar. Walking around I found six bottles of very expensive drink on the way. Mum got up worried, and all Cathy would say was "whoops!" and she then went to sleep it off in bed under her trusty doona.

A while later, down Cathy came... sore and sorry and told me she had rolled into the gutter and couldn't get up. There was no bloody truck that had hit her... oh Cathy!!!

Besides all her fun she topped the state in nursing. I was so proud of her that night. I cried tears of joy, as to me she'd beat the anxiety and smashed it out of the park. She was a very hard-working nurse and I now see, like me, healing others was also healing herself.

She finally fell in love with a top guy and they bought their first house in Maryland. Her biggest dream was to become a mother. Sadly, that could never be. They had a few goes at IVF—the second one was a success. Oh, how happy we all were. I was pregnant with what was to become my beautiful daughter, Cody. We both had the same due dates or very close. Wow dreams come true. Cathy got a belly very quick and told the world it was twins. She was in maternity dresses at six weeks.

We both set off for our scans on the same day, so excited. When I hadn't heard from her or Mum, I had a bad feeling. I picked up the phone shaking as I somehow just 'knew" in my heart. Mum answered the phone and was crying and I could hear smashing and screaming in the background. Cathy was pregnant with twins, but their little hearts had stopped beating a few weeks before. My heart sunk... How? Why? my poor Big Sis. Life wasn't playing fair for my Big Sis.

Cathy put all her love into my children after this. When I had Cody, it was so ironic she was working in the same hospital the same time I got my little girl. I could not help but feel guilty. I wanted her to at least have the first little girl in the family, but that was not to be. Cathy was so good with my children and took them on lots of fun times out. She told me one day that she broke into Charlestown Square and took them roller blading all night. I believed this as I wouldn't put anything past my big Sis, especially knowing all the shenanigans she'd get up to. The kids went along with it for years and I'm easily convinced but I had my doubts.

Cathy moved on and left that marriage. She then announced to us she was madly in love with a girl she had met, and informed us all she was bisexual. This was not a good relationship at all, and she made a very good first attempt to take herself home (end her life). She cut her wrists very well, she knew where and how to cut them, from her nursing.

I'll never forget Mum bringing her home, I was so scared I could have lost her. Again, I slept or pretended to while she cried all night. She told me she was mad and did not want to be saved. She told me "life was just too hard for her" and she did not feel she was meant for this world. I said "Cathy, you are my hero, look at all you have achieved. Promise me you will never leave me Sis?".

Mum had the house extended and we had a new room out the back near the sunroom. I felt so much change in the house when the extensions were built. They cracked the concrete driveway and it was like they opened a burial ground. The energy was so bad. By now I had really locked into feeling energy and spirit around me.

I sat in the loungeroom one night with headphones on crying for her so she would not see me. I felt a dark energy come and sit in front of me, it was like it was staring me down. I threw the headphones down and ran out to the family.

That night in bed Cathy had finally given in to exhaustion. She was sound asleep. I felt something come up over the blankets. It felt like it was pushing down on me. I hid under the blankets unable to move. Next thing I heard the wardrobe doors open. No way! they were hard to open as they were big wooden doors.

Sure enough they were open. That was it, I ran into Mum and told her. Sadly, my life of spirit stories had got old and she said "Honey go back to bed, you're just upset over Cathy".

So finally, the spirits showed themselves to others in that house. So many people just would not stay there. Mum worked in VideoEzy for many years after we left, and she has been told that many families had also some pretty scary times in that house. So I was definitely not the only one that felt the presence of spirit in that house. At least it validated what I'd always known.

Cathy moved on from her girlfriend and met a guy at the sailing club. By now she was a trophy wife sort of girl. Such a huge change, as I said you just never knew what or who you would get with her. They bought and did up a beautiful house at Redhead. She would be the belle of the ball every street Christmas party in her red dresses.

Cathy loved the snow, and would live on near nothing to look good when she was on the slopes. This is when her Bulimia kicked in big time and to add to that, her love of painkillers to knock herself out, not be hungry and to numb herself to the reality of her world. My red lights were back flashing big time. She would ring me, and would be off her face on god knows what. One day she took herself shopping like this. She lost her car, so she got a taxi home, or tried to. No mobile phones in those days—so they pulled over at a phone booth and the driver got her address.

∾ ∾ ∾

That marriage came to an end and she decided girls were definitely her thing. She moved to Summerland Point—oh she had a ball in the gay scene. She stayed up all night partying and went under the blankets every now and then when her body gave in—she pushed her body to breakdown again. Mum lived close by, and one day Cathy rang and said she could not live like this anymore. To my poor Mum's horror when they got there, she had the car set up to gas herself.

It was time to act.

We got her to the doctors, and she was happy to go into rehab. She had moved in with Mum so with all her things there, she set off to rehab for the first time. She was in her element there, sadly—she got all the attention and drugs she wanted. I went to talk to her doctor, and he said, till she is ready to give them up we can't help. I hated it there but there was nothing any of us could do.

She was in there a few months; she finally did get straight with a lot of hard work. Sadly, the Cathy they sent home was a shell of the Cathy we all knew. All she did was sleep, eat and purge.

As I sit and write this, I ask her if its okay to share this much. She tells me 'Ellen, if its saves one person share it all'.

There is so much more I just can't share. She was in and out of rehab and seeing doctors for so long. They would fix her, and she would break. Her most remembered rehab was the one at Bondi. Wow did she bluff them. We could not contact her for six weeks. It was so hard, but nice to know she was safe.

We finally got a call saying we could go and see her, so Mum, Cody and I headed down the next day. They said she was doing so well she would be graduating and able to leave ahead of time. It was no surprise to me they loved her so much that they had offered her a job. After being with her for an hour I could see the mask she had on.

I went and spoke with the head doctor, I said that is not my sister she is putting on a huge act. They said they knew their job and that she was doing great and this was a full recovery this time as she was ready. Oh really? fair enough I thought... I knew my sister well and I knew she was not back.

So, the next day at lunch time she rang me. One of her best this one, 'Hi Ellen, we are having a great day out".

"Okay Cathy, who is having a great day out and where are you?' I asked.

"We are about to get on the Manly Ferry", she replied. This was not good—she had busted about ten of them out, got them drugs, alcohol, smokes and chocolate to go. They were all high as kites.

I contacted the rehab centre as soon as I got them off the phone. She took them all back when it was dark. Clever girl, she threw a heap of supplies she had got them, to grab later. She was in for a big few day with the stash she'd hidden away. Thankfully they outsmarted her this time and found them all. I must say it was so funny, once I knew she was safe. So, Doc, I was right, she was the chameleon of chameleons, my big sis.

It was a few more months before she did come home, she was so quiet and sad—I hated it. My sis was lost, life was just too hard in this lifetime for her. She rode the roller coaster of borderline personality disorder for a long time after that.

I had an overwhelming premonition for a month I could not kick. I knew something bad was going to happen as I always get déjà vu flat out before something big happens in my life. Like spirit is preparing me and showing me before and maybe after but they keep the 'after' from me and bring it in slow.

A few weeks earlier she had sent me a card that is very dear to me now, saying 'I was the sunshine in her every day'... and my stomach turned.

CHAPTER 7

The Unthinkable

So, the unthinkable happened. You always think things will never happen to you until it does... and it changed my life forever.

The last time I saw my Big Sis she called in the morning on her way out for the day. Cathy sat on the arm of my lounge—she knew that pissed me off.

That day though I smiled and went and got her some money. I said "Cathy go have a fun day".

She said "what is this for?"

I said "just because I love you".

She left with that huge smile that I'll never see again.

We were getting a new kitchen the next day—finally, after years of curtains for doors—I was busy most of the day. As the afternoon came, I was struck down with the worst migraine I've ever had in my life.

I ran a bath and laid in it for hours. Cody had gone out for the night, so I gave in to it.

Cathy started texting me about 5pm, that afternoon that she had a fight and was really upset. She was close by, so I said

"Cathy come to mine, please". I had run to her so many times with these texts, so it was like the boy who cried wolf.

She kept texting so I tried to ring her.

She wouldn't answer, my head was so bad I could not get to her and told her again to come down to me.

She told me she had smashed the house and was so over her life.

My alarm bells rang, as she had told me one day, she would do this and then kill herself.

I tried and tried to ring her. She texted back she didn't feel like talking. I asked her what she had done, and she told me what she'd done. She told me a different story and did well, so it threw me off for a bit.

I texted my other sister and she said Cathy had also been texting her. She was fine and she was going back to rehab the next day and could they take her?

She told me to calm down as I tend to over-think with my gift—it's hard to know what is a message from Spirit and what is my OCD thinking.

I got one final text saying 'sorry Sis, I've calmed down' and texted to make sure she could get to rehab the next day.

With that she bluffed me for the first time.

I got this urgent feeling I had to go up and check on her about nine that night. Greg and I both went up there and knocked and knocked—no answer.

I said "she may be asleep as she'd had a few drinks and would be upset and knocked out". We went home and I went to bed eager to talk to her in the morning.

Not long after I went to bed, I felt her leave this lifetime.

I went to the back gate and said 'fly free at last Cathy, I love you'.

Nothing could ever prepare me for the next morning. I woke, sat up and said "Greg, Cathy is dead. I need to find her". I said

I'm going up to the house she was staying at. He wouldn't let me go and went up on his own. He came home–ashen grey.

He said "Honey she's not there, but she has smashed the house up bad".

Her mind had finally snapped. I rang and rang her phone— no answer, and my instinct told me, she was there. I had to go there. By then there was a few of us at her place. I just remember saying "The shed... oh no!... the shed".

The next thing I remember was screaming and people pushing me away from the shed. My beautiful big sister had finally succeeded to do what she had tried to do so many times.

Her soul was free.

My sister was gone.

I was in shock so bad and I had to now go and tell my Mum.

Greg tried to just get me to go with him to Mum's place but I was on auto pilot. I will never forget the scream on the other end of the phone that day. I was already dressed and I dressed myself in another outfit over the one I had on. I went down to my eldest son's room and said, 'Aunty Cathy's killed herself and I need to go to Nan'. My poor son, he loved her so much — I just ran off in shock. So many mistakes that day but the shock of finding her was too much to take in. I thought "I am the oldest now and must look after everyone".

If I could turn back time, would I have stopped her that night? I really don't know, as I know her soul is now free. She talks to me and works with me every day. She tells me she chose to stay and not come back this time as she is a suicide watcher and proud to still be a healer.

We played the Nat King Cole song *Unforgettable* at her funeral... and she most definitely was.

CHAPTER 8

My Rollercoaster ride down into the Dark Rabbit Hole

How I kept going for the next few days, weeks, months I'll never really know. There were people in and out—and all I wanted was to curl up and die. One day they all left me. I must have told Greg I wanted to be alone. He came home and kept an eye on me but let me be. I got up the next morning and asked if his sisters had been and packed all my new kitchen. He said no, you had the music full blast singing and cleaning all day.

Everyone went back to their own lives and work. I would get up, get my kids to school, and clean the house, as my OCD can't stand a dirty house. Then I would sit in my wardrobe and rock all day till they began to come home. Then on with my mask. I would come and look after everyone—as that was my job.

I started taking pain killers to knock myself out, so I didn't have to think or feel anything. I ate and purged all day while no one was there to see me. Cathy had taught me well how to do this and clean up, so no one knew. Of a weekend I drank myself to the point of blackouts. At the end of a night drinking, I would get so sad I would scratch my skin till it bled to let the pain out.

Before Cathy took herself home, I had taken a few too many tablets when I was drinking one night as I thought life would be better without me. A few months before she left us, I had been depressed for months. I sat on my floor with enough tablets to get me out of this world and looked to the sky and said "my father in heaven come and get me now". I wanted to be in his arms, the arms I never knew, where I thought I would be safe.

Suddenly, I snapped out of it thinking 'my baby girl would be first home and would find me'.

The next thing I knew, I was struck by the most beautiful feeling I had ever felt. Seems the big man himself had come to save me. I rang a Christian friend and the next I knew I was a born-again Christian. I feel God was preparing to carry me through losing Cathy. It did and I guess that's why he kept me here, to show how low we can go and how much we can heal.

Life went on like a roller coaster, so many ups and downs. I had my three beautiful children, so I had to keep going. I wish I could change some of the things they saw in life. I can't. I can only hope they love me as much as I love them. If it was not for them, I really don't know if I would be here—that's for sure.

As I sit and write today, I'm in Foster and they are all on my mind, as the state is in catastrophic fire danger. I am sending my protection to them and all involved in the fires. As a psychic I must make sure my mind does not get ahead too far or see things that may not be. You see all the posts on Facebook and the news sets us off.

For the week before I came up, I had a bad feeling. I had seen these fires and when Greg got the concreting job, he feared rain. I said "no, I can smell the fires". With a few friends voicing their worry, I built it up way too far. I walked and grounded myself and took back my red shoes. When I step into my red shoes, they take me into my power and magic place. I have to say though—I was had got myself into a real state of anxiety.

I was an aged care nurse for a while and really impressed myself with my knowledge of medical terminology. I loved working with the dementia patients. It was in my soul to heal and I was loving this part of my life journey. It was all fine and well till I had to start writing reports for the doctor to see. My fear of people saying I can't spell was huge. My step dad used to call me dumb all the time and it stuck so bad.

I also had a huge fear of finding a client passed—funny that, as I now talk with them from the other side every day. I ended up getting more hours in the kitchen and felt safe there. This I would regret for many years, the healer in me was fighting to come out and play. I left there after seven years as I had enough of missing so much of my kids lives working night and afternoon shifts.

I worked cleaning a motel not far from home until Greg got laid off at Christmas time. The company he worked for went broke. So, that is when he built our company Elcon Civil. Greg bought me a computer and I taught myself to run the office. It was on the computer I finally found a group for people who are left after suicide. I would sit up all night at times talking to people like me, lost with no place to turn.

There was nowhere to go back then—it was so hard having no where to turn to or someone to reach out to when I felt so alone.

Sadly, I would go out and people would judge Cathy and say how cruel she was to do this to me. Sorry—if a person had cancer and they took their life they would be called brave, yet a person with depression, borderline personality disorder and schizophrenia was a coward? Sadly that's a life sentence as well.

I loved this group and I would talk with and help many as I was healing myself. One of the counsellors on the group asked me if I was a counsellor? I said no and she said well you need to go study girl; you have a gift. It appears I do, but study was not needed, spirit was standing by waiting.

My roller coaster took the best high ever when Josh and Tanya announced I was about to become a grandmother. The best role ever - this was a ride I was happy to be on.

CHAPTER 9

Grammy Time

I decided I was not going to be Nan or Grandma, I was Grammy. My life took another turn. I was blessed to be with Tanya and Josh while my beautiful Layla entered the world. I was told the love for grand kids was amazing although I felt I could never love them like I love my own children.

Let me tell you, when that little face was looking up at me in my arms, my whole world became magical again. My Layla Rose—my first grandchild. The world stood still while I soaked in her gorgeous features.

Tanya was nursing so Layla became a huge part of my world, working from home allowed me to have her while Mummy went to work. I finally found a focus again. My inner child went nuts playing and laughing all day. She gave us a few big health scares, so she kept me in my red shoes doing the worry dance.

A few years later, as Aarron was about to go to Europe for a year, Shell came in, walked down my hallway, and I said "oh my god... you're pregnant!'. I was blessed to share so much of the pregnancy with her and her mother, as Daddy still went overseas for six months. I'll never forget the day we headed off for the scan to tell us what they were having. It was obvious to the whole room, and cheers of joy—it was our first little boy... I'm still trying to see that extra boy bit on the scan!

His Daddy came home, and they gave me the most beautiful soul—my Bodie Charles. Just when you think life can't get better along comes another beautiful grandchild. There is nothing better than a night in with my grand-kids. I could share all my fairy tales again and bring them to life all over again. I could show them my fairies and we could live in my magic world. Down my magic rabbit hole, we would go and leave the world behind us. They love it when we go there.

My next miracle was his little sister, Miss Mayah Grace, a new sister for Bodie and little princess for Mummy and Daddy. She was just adorable and had her Daddy wrapped around his little finger in no time. She had masses of black hair and big chubby cheeks, just like him as a baby. His nickname when he plays football is Chopper. She did not take long to prove she had a spot in this world and quickly earned herself some sass now she is getting older.

Another princess with my prince when I had them all. My life really was a magic carpet ride with them by my side.

Not long after Mayah I got a phone call. Layla got on the phone first and said 'Merry Christmas Grammy, I'm getting a little brother or sister'. It went straight over the top of my head and I said, 'Wow that's so good honey'. Josh got on the phone and said 'Mum did you not hear Layla', I heard what she had said and it hit me. I started screaming with joy, what a Christmas miracle this was—as Tanya was a few months along and hid it from us, so she could tell her Mum while up at Noosa visiting with her.

So, it was not that long before my beautiful Evie Jade came into the world screaming, and kept doing so for a good few months. She is definitely a strong-willed girl that one. She was so headstrong, when the poor little girl was sick, she would just scream and scream. She did not like crowds and had a mind of her own. Once she started day care the change was unbelievable. She was so eager to learn and so social. She loves the stage like Layla and Mayah, my tiny dancers. My heart is so full of pride when I watch them all.

Evie seemed to be born with my gift, I think Bodie has it as well, but Evie is more vocal about it. When its story time with them her eyes lock into mine. Of a night they all love Reiki then a good fairy tale with them all in it. They giggle with joy when it comes to their part. Then the magic sleep fairies come and sprinkle purple fairy dust in their eyes and off to fairy dream land they go. One night I heard this loud bang in the middle of the night. I ran to Evie and found her sitting on the floor with her eyes still closed, she said "Grammy I did not open them so I would have fairy dreams and I ran into the door". Bless her little soul.

She went home and started telling her Mum all these things that would come true. When asked how she knew it all she said "Grammy charges me up, I look in her eyes and I get magic powers off her". I took note while telling her own fairy tale last time I had her and yes, her eyes were so fixed on mine just as she'd said.

Then along came Mr Lennox James—Mr Personality—and one tough little dude, that was definitely shown at his entry into this lifetime. He was already in fight mode in the womb, he really should not have made it here. Michelle had *Placenta Increta*, she went into labour two days before his due date for her caesarean, in true form he doesn't like to have to wait.

This very exciting time turned into a big nightmare. We were called to meet our new little man and her Mum and I were so excited. When we got there the nurse said there had been a complication and we needed to talk to Aarron. He was in with Lennox and we could not get anyone to tell us a thing. Michelle's Mum went into mother mode and said something is very wrong here. Finally, Aarron came out with the news—they had cut the placenta and she'd had a bleed—they had taken her to surgery, but all should be fine.

Aarron was hungry so we went and got him tea. I parked in the quick park and her Mum ran it up to him. She came running back, ashen grey and crying. "We need to go up and help Aarron with the baby as Michelle is not good". We went up and there was this tiny little man crying his tiny eyes out. I said 'Aarron, take your shirt off and put him on your chest for him to feel your skin'. I walked over towards them. He said "Mum stop, you can't see him... Michelle hasn't yet". So he put this tiny little soul on his chest and the baby calmed.

It was hours before the doctor came in and said we saved her, we had to give her a full hysterectomy, but we stopped the bleeding. I said oh my God she is so young, she was only twenty-three, he glared at me and said "she's alive".

We had no idea as no one could tell us anything, he said they lost her a few times and they had to bring her back a few times. She had bled so much. Silence filled the room and we were frozen with fear for her.

She was in intensive care and on life support. I decided it was best for me to leave her with her mother and Aarron. I don't even remember driving home or what time it was. Not long after I got home her Mum rang me and told me she was holding on, but they had to give her so much blood and they thought they had broken her ribs resuscitating her. No words came from me that night, I lay and prayed in silence all night.

The next morning, I was so happy and shocked to find out

that Shell was out of ICU and we could go in and meet our little hero. It turns out if he did not come early, we would have lost them both. He saved his Mummy's life. He calls her his princess and she says he is her prince.

∾ ∾ ∾

As I sit here and write this, I have another tiny dancer safe and sound waiting to come into our world—she is a blessing I did not expect, my heart is just so full of love for her already. I keep seeing the most beautiful big brown eyes. I can't wait to see if they belong to her.

This will make six little cherubs for me to share my magic with. My biggest wish is "don't take the magic of the world away from the children". Many kids see as I did, and it was so confusing for me trying to understand why I was being told to stop sharing the messages I was given - to stop my magic. After all these years I can finally bathe in my magic Grammy world and have the chance to share it with my Grandies.

CHAPTER 10

Down the Magic Rabbit Hole

As I've said before, I had this gift at a young age. To me I knew no different. It's like "the knowing" I would call it.

I always just knew when things were going to happen. I loved to run and share it with Mum and Cathy, and I guess anyone who would listen. I still do —I just can't hold back if Spirit has a message for me to deliver, and I guess now I do like to let people know what I have become. Never in my wildest dreams did I think it would bring me this far.

A lot of my younger life I can remember that whenever I felt fear, I would go down my magic rabbit hole. I'd close my eyes and see what made me feel safe and happy, it helped sooth and calm me—like a form of my own meditation—I taught myself how to do this at a young age. I guess way back then, it was my guides and passed loved one's way of protecting me.

As a child I loved Alice in Wonderland - especially the Mad Hatter's Tea Party. The Cheshire Cat would be Cathy; and I would try to take her into my world to protect us both—even though she didn't know it. Even now as I write this, it's Spirit showing me how clever I was back then. If I shut out the bad and think good, it changes the energy around me.

Later in life I studied to become a Reiki Master and learnt we are made up of energy— if it all resonates and we are positive, we receive positive. If we let negative get a hold of us, we can get stuck there as it grows and grows—it eats away at our subconscious mind.

If we feed it—we seem to fall into another hole - the dark hole. As a child it would feel like I would go to play with the big, bad witch—she is hard to get away from and my fear would build and build. She feeds your mind poison that keeps you tired and steals away what strength you have to climb your way out of that dark place.

With Cathy in the room telling me "the bad man is coming" or 'the green ghost', I would try and dig deeper and be brave at times instead of going to my magic place. One night I was so scared and felt so stuck—I could hear men outside— I was frozen. I eventually found the strength to pull myself out of there. To my horror, my hair was caught on the bed and I couldn't free myself and Cathy had gone to sleep. I was trapped... I remember breathing quickly and feeling out of control of my body. It was horrible. To this day I hate small places and as a child, after this experience, I would not climb under my bed.

∞ ∞ ∞

I had to have an MRI the other month and it was a huge fear for me. Again as we do with anxiety—I fed it big time. Fear of what's ahead before we face it. With the help of two beautiful Reiki Masters—and a lot of meditating (and maybe a sedating drug), I faced my fear head on and beat it.

It's very common for the subconscious mind to hold on to these memories and where phobias come from. I say the subconscious mind is our soul—we may even hold onto fears from other lives—I know I do—and it was a relief to have this one validated in a reading a while back.

∽∽ ∽∽ ∽∽

In another lifetime I was an American Indian. I was a twin in this lifetime and I was the cheeky monkey of us both. Always stirring my sister in this lifetime. I had a lot of fun and ran wild. While travelling on Route 66 with Greg in March he noticed I was not singing or talking—that's so not normal for me.

I was so drawn in by the land—I could not believe it. I could feel myself in this other life running around and riding around on my horse there. I felt free and peaceful.

I was shown by Spirit, as we got close to the Grand Canyon—that I fell backwards into it—stirring my sister big time. I was six and my life in that lifetime ended there. Anyone that knows me knows I can't stand snakes and escalators—I feel like I'm falling backwards—if they move or turn, I feel like I need to sit down. Hate is a big word but I hate them and heights so bloody bad. Now I finally understood why.

When I became a Reiki Master, I went to Oakdale Farm for Evie's birthday party. We were walking to the big shed with the kids and Josh. I said "there are no snakes in this show hey?". With a funny smirk he said "no Mum".

The kids were looking at a big container the farmhand was carrying next to me. Just as the show started I learned it had one h-u-g-e python in it! I tried to climb into the bag of the lady sitting next to me. I looked to see if I could jump off the back of the grandstand—nope. I was stuck.

My fear was next level. Panic-attack me off!! As I looked, I could see the show had stopped and the attention had turned to me... oops!

Next thing I hear in my head 'fear is fear of fear itself'... Bam! so I take it up a level— my grand-kids were watching this—so you know what I said? "I'm going to pat that snake on the way out".

Oh my god... where did these words come from?

Was that my mouth?

Did I say it or think it?

A friend that was with us said, "you know what? if you pat it, I will".

Okay... now I'm really stuffed.

True to Ellen form—I never back out—I did it! I still cringe when I think of it but I did it. I love to conquer my fears now. Nothing is going to beat me again.

∞ ∞ ∞

I'm not saying fear is not good—we need to feel good and bad, that's for sure. That's why fairy tales are good. Children learn through them—not to eat the poison apple, or to go near the bad witch—even though some witches are good.

Some fears can be beaten—it can break a hold on you—some can't. I struggle to beat my fear of tight spaces.

As I got older my anxiety grew—it really got a big hold on me. I didn't want to go out and have fun anymore. For me to go out, I would get very drunk—that was not a good thing for me. I seemed like I was the life of the party and I never shut up. I thought everyone wanted to hear my dragged-out stories to keep their attention and I was a huge attention seeker! This is where my psychic ability came in handy.

I found the more I drank the more messages from Spirit flowed.

In the ladies bathroom I would have them lining up for messages. I would deliver some great messages when I was drinking–I must say, but the first thing I learned in my spiritual development classes was 'never mix spirits with Spirit'.

After my friends or family had a well-earned rest from my verbal diarrhoea, they would say "oh no... Ellen must be reading in the ladies bathroom again!" especially when I didn't come back. It was all fun until I got home—the room would spin and I'd throw up—then head for the bath and scratch myself until I bled, to let the pain out. I'd then wash and wash and wash, to wash the drink away. Like Cathy, I would spend the next day in bed and not want to talk to anyone.

I would take tablets and knock myself out.

I tried to give up a few times, but I guess the drink that always started a good night down the magic rabbit hole, inevitably delivered me into a dark, depressed hole the next day. My anxiety would go through the roof as I would be so worried I had said something wrong.

Back in the day I also loved my smokes. Through the day they tasted like shit, but they calmed my nerves... but put them with a drink and I would smoke a packet in a night. I started to find my mind waking me up at 3 am every morning for a smoke with a coffee and somehow, I would manage to go back to sleep afterwards but... it really was time to kick this in the butt so to speak. I attempted quitting a few times, even tried hypnotherapy. I finally said I will have my last smoke on my birthday five years ago... and succeeded!

∾∾ ∾∾ ∾∾

Addiction is how we drive that subconscious mind. A huge power source we need to rewire at times—if only I had Reiki back then.

I found I went from one addiction to another—so no smokes equals more food which equals bulimia. I had named my bulimia: Bella. Geez... I even gave her a name - she liked that and, it happened to be a name I liked. So why not feed it some more.

I put on over ten kilograms fast – again after giving up. This caused major back pain so was prescribed very strong pain killers... Bonus! another addiction covered!

I was told to rest as much as I needed. I grabbed that opportunity to mean I could lay and eat and sleep all day and knock myself out again in the evening. Life was good!

I didn't feel much stress now in my drugged state of bliss. I didn't have to go out as much. I would still drink of a weekend—and how I woke up some mornings I will never know, as at the end of the night I would pop a pain killer on top of drinking so as not to wake with a headache.

It was fun for a while, but then I started to get mentally stronger and wanted my weight off for my son's wedding.

When I commit—I'm all in. I went on shakes and lost twenty kilograms before the big day. I felt so in control as my image and how I look, is a huge thing to me. I've never liked who I saw in the mirror. I picked the hell out of her. If I was given a compliment, I would answer back with a negative instead of a thank you.

I would live in this negative mindset for so many years—this was the life I seemed to think I deserved... boy was I so wrong. Looking back now I think '... if only I knew all this so many years ago'.

The incredible thing is — if I didn't break, would I be here working so hard to support others and embrace who I am? It's true - when the bone breaks it grows back stronger— all the pain I've faced in my life has led me to the path I now walk.

∾ ∾ ∾

The subconscious mind is the network to so much in our physical bodies, we need to be careful we don't blow a few fuses. Now when I give Reiki it feels like I'm hot wiring the car so to speak. So you can think of your life journey just like you're driving a car. You take the wheel and controls of your journeys— you steer yourself through the twists, turns, ups, downs and potholes of life. Some corners are easy to navigate and others throw you off into the gravel. They were all part of your life journey to get you to this exact point in your life. It was all mapped out ahead for you... and you didn't even know it.

I know in my own journey I kept getting my 'car' stuck in reverse.

So, imagine you've put the car in reverse and you're backing into a fire.

Would you not choose to simply go forward and get the hell out of there? of course you would! So why do many people live their lives staring in the rearview mirror of their past, and stuck in the fire where they got burnt?

Sadly, because they think it's what they deserve—when in fact they need help with someone to show them how to accelerate and leave it there - to leave it behind.

My spiritual healing finally showed me how to get in my magic red shoes and slam the accelerator forward at full speed – with no fear.

Of course you'd go forward, right?

Yet I want to know why we keep going back to the past?

So many times in my journey I had to face and work through

that past. I know now I've been back to those dark holes enough – so it's time to heal others, the way I healed myself and to be there for those who have lost someone they love.

Just today my Mother said, "Ellen you know when Cathy took her life, I rang a suicide support line and I got a message saying - 'sorry we are on holidays please ring back in a fortnight'."

I know many beautiful people that went to get help so many times, and were sent home and told, 'take these drugs and sleep... your mind is tired'. I also know two men that gave up and chose to just take themselves 'home' by ending their lives.

∽ ∽ ∽

There is so much more help at hand now but for some that may never be enough. My aim in life is to be there for as many people as I can. To tell the raw truth of where I have been. To go out of my comfort zone and help in any way I can.

I'll give them their own magic red shoes but they need to learn how to dance in them on their own.

I don't teach anything too hard for them to take in – as their minds are too fragile when we start our journey of healing together. So it's like a fairy-tale — it's magic. It's their yellow brick road—so we fix the things that would stop them from moving forward—my blessing is when I see them in their shoes dancing out the gate.

My job is done... their life has just begun.

CHAPTER 11

Finding my Red Shoes

I found myself living in a shop called Reflections Within—Spirit was calling me home. I love to go over there and chat to the girls. I love the crystals, and the magic seemed to come back to life in me whenever I was there.

When they would talk, I felt at home. I could laugh and tell them funny things that had happened that I didn't want to share with others. They got me—I felt comfortable. I told them how I could talk with spirit and pass on messages all my life. They found it normal... and I found it home.

Every time I went out into crowds I started to feel all over the place—I would be happy and then bam... I could sit and cry or scream at people. I would go into the shop on the way home and ground myself and the crystal energy would soothe my soul.

My favourite crystal is tourmaline for my line of work and I sing its praises daily. It's the only crystal that cleanses itself, as well negative energy. I love my crystals and work with them daily. Those who know me know to never call them rocks or stones to me because they are a live energy—they deserve a better name. They are magic to me.

The pull was getting so strong and I found myself always having answers to questions for people, especially when I was out and about.

It was my birthday and my daughter had booked us into the casino in Tasmania for two nights, so I left in a great mood. On this trip I fell in love with nature and mother earth. As we were driving, I started to look at the trees like I never had before and I've always been totally obsessed with waterfalls, if I hear one, I just start running till I reach the magnificence of her.

We visited Port Arthur for the day and I had been warned to put white light protection around me and take some crystals for my energy. Let's say that didn't work at all. Greg dropped me in the carpark to go park the car. I started to fall forward—it was a horrible feeling as I hate not being in control of my body, it makes me anxious. I didn't tell him as I feel I'm always whinging when we are away, as I struggle with anxiety when on holidays.

Halfway around the tour at Port Arthur and I felt an anger I had never felt in my life. I just wanted to punch people that were getting in my road. On the drive back to the casino I felt that if I had a knife, I could stab someone and no matter what, this feeling stayed with me for a long time. The energy of the place had got under my psychic skin and it wasn't pleasant.

When I returned home, Max had organised a Wellbeing Fair. I just loved to go and look at all the readers in the big room and think how much I would love to be in there. I had turned my gift on and off for so many years. Not because I did not want to use it, because I thought people would not believe me or think I was crazy. Well, it turns out I'm okay being a bit bat shit, witchy poo crazy and love it.

As I walked in, I said to Max, "I think I should become a psychic", she laughed and said "...about bloody time Ellen!". She gave me the name of a great teacher and that was it.

Time to do what I wanted in my heart for so many years.

I walked around the stalls feeling like this was my world. I felt really dizzy suddenly and nearly walked out and later learned this was spirit. I can feel them and now can tell spirit energy... and that day the place was jam packed full. I went out to watch Nic on stage and I thought how cool this would be to do this.

When I walked in, I went to sit at the front and I heard like a voice in my head say 'spirit will find you sit at the back'. Nic started asking lots of questions that all added up for me. The next thing she walked up to me and the main thing I remember was "girl you need to sort your stomach problems out as you are a healer and need to get to work with spirit".

BAM! that was the word 'healer' ...that was the key word.

I didn't just want to read... I wanted to heal. Maybe it could all tie in? I floated out of there with my teachers name in my pocket and my head focused on me for once. I decided I'm going for it! then as I walked around the stalls two stall-holders with a gift said to me, "you are going to be a well-known healer". Who me? wow is this real? One even gave me a gift and said "...and when you are a healer, come back and find me, I could use you".

My heart turned on that day... I was like a beagle on a scent—I had to do this. So, Monday I rang and booked myself into a six-week beginners development class. I came home and told the family I was going to do classes to learn how to use this gift—I didn't quite receive the reception I was hoping for—but I had to do this for me.

The night before I started class I caught up with my daughter Cody, she said "Mum what do you hope to get out of this?"

Straight away I said, "healing people".

∾∾ ∾∾ ∾∾

Never did I dream that day would lead me to where I am today. I was anxious and excited all at once. I was fighting anxiety big time around the time I started class. As soon as I walked in the door, I felt dizzy again... oh no what is this? is this a panic attack? I wanted to run out and feel the safety of home again but I wasn't going to let anxiety steal this away from me. I wanted it so badly.

I didn't have to wait long before five more beautiful souls walked into the room—all eager to learn what to do with their gifts as well and in their own ways. I still see some of them and some of them have grown and used their gifts in their own ways. Such special earth angels I'm blessed they are in my life.

We were taken into another room where we were to learn how to use this gift we had. Within two minutes I was sweating so bad I thought I would faint. Looking around the room everyone else seemed fine. It wasn't a hot night and I was soon that to learn to welcome spirit, your body temp goes up as they enter the room.

We were all sitting in a circle and I guess my spirit guides were happy to put me to work as soon as I sat down. In an instant I was hot and dizzy and again wanting to run. They must have thought 'what is this girl doing?' as there was no way I could sit still. We were taught so much on that first night and strangely I felt I had been there and learnt it all before.

Damn it was good to sit and listen to like-minded people. I finally felt in my life that I fitted in. Our teacher guided us into a meditation to find our guides—I was so excited.

My guide appeared as a boxer dog beside me—not what I wanted. As we all came out of meditation our teacher asked us if we got a guide... and better still a name? Most did well. She got to me and I said, "I got a dog, like am I the dog whisperer".

The room erupted in laughter and My teacher laughed and said, "Ellen maybe this dog is connected to someone and wants to bring through a message to you?".

Well, I hope so—I wasn't really wanting a dog as my guide lol... sorry to this beautiful creature but I was a bit disappointed.

Driving home that night, I was proud that I made it and didn't run from my anxiety—I saw the dog again too... okay I get it! The penny dropped... this was Sharon's dog! Shaz was letting me know she was there beside me!

She sure made her presence felt from then on, over and over. We would be doing class, and everyone would pick up on things that were her. We all had to give a name each week of a loved one, and each of us in the class had to channel what we could pick up on the person they had written down.

On my way home feeling very proud of what I had channelled with the help of Allan and their Spirit, I was thinking I'll use my grandmother. I heard, *'no you will not McInerny, you will use me!'*.

A week later it was my turn. Sharon Forbes—and off they went. They all got so much on her so quickly. I could feel her floating around the room. It was so hot in there that night.

Even my teacher seemed to feel her strongly, she quickly learned that Shaz liked to teach—that was her job in life, and she seemed to think she had to be there in all our lessons.

At a Psychic Fair months later, my teacher was doing platform, she picked up my grandmother and was giving me some amazing messages I needed at the time.

She then looked at me funny and said, "Ellen we will talk about this later".

I was not reading at this Fair, so I went off to look around. I must say my heart was beating double-time as my mother was having another cancer scare at the time. As soon as I saw my teacher having lunch I ran up and said, "please tell me all is okay?".

She laughed and said, "Shaz came in all dressed up ready for a good chat"... phew! I should have known.

So, every second Tuesday I went in and learned and grew in my gift I was blessed with at birth. It was like being reborn, it was my heart calling. Finally, my six weeks course came to an end. Finally, I fit in and it all added up.

The last night we had to all take our cards and read the teacher, I was so nervous. I watched the others have their turn, and they all read with a beautiful flow. My turn came and the nerves took over big time. I had my angel cards and she drew five. I opened my book and read each card. She looked at me and said "Ellen next time you buy a pack of cards, when you get the book, sit on it". Me being thick as a brick thought, *'but how will I know what each card means?'*.

Then she said two words I took honour in hearing and owning... "Ellen you are a psychic clairvoyant. You don't need books—use your gift". Instead of feeling like I didn't do as well as the others—I floated out of there owning my new title in life, that I'd had all along.

CHAPTER 12

Finding the Gift of Reiki

In the middle of meditation one day to bring Spirit in I heard 'reiki'. Me being me, spoke without thinking to my teacher, 'what is reiki?' With a look of please be quiet, she said "we will talk after class".

It turned out her partner was a master, so it all fell into place. After that class one of the gentlest souls I ever met, walked me to my car. On the way she explained she did Reiki and was about to do her Master's degree.

Her words were, "…it's just beautiful, so beautiful"

I had no idea and did not even Google it. Before I knew it, I was at my Level One Reiki class. Well, if I thought I fit in the other class, this one I was being poured with light and love. My classmates were such beautiful souls. The same house yet such a different flowing energy.

As I sat there, I was like a human sponge. I hate study or being taught but this was just so interesting just in the first part of learning the symbols and energy exchange that we need to resonate and balance to heal others. Mind you I never knew we are energy, so it was so interesting.

Reiki is a form of alternative medicine called - energy healing. Reiki practitioners use a form called palm healing, hands on healing, through which universal energy is said to be transferred through the palms of the practitioner to the patient in order to encourage emotional and physical healing.

So, we learned our first symbols for level one. Cho Ku Rei is the power symbol. Sei Ho Ki the emotional symbol. Hon Sha Ze Sho Nen, distance healing. Dia Ko Myo the master symbol.

So much excitement was building at lunch as we had our attunement after the break. Our master had not eaten as they fast for this special gift to be passed on. It was time. We were taken from the room one by one for a moment that would change my life from that day forward.

I sat in the chair closed my eyes and smack! a massive panic attack— or so it felt. I heard my Masters voice change, his hands upon my shoulders he said, "Its okay child". I was calm. I swear I saw God that day standing with his arms out to me. I knew he was giving me my own symbols that we don't get to know. It was a feeling of light and love I had never felt before.

When it was finished, my hands were so warm and tingling. The Master had said "...when we finish, please walk back into the front room and start to share Reiki with one of the classmates on the bed". I remember clearly, he said I don't talk from the start to the end of the attunements. Yet as I opened my eyes he said "welcome home" and his hand gestured. I went out the back to ground.

The tears flowed, the light of my heart had been lit, I was home at last. I returned to the room and proceeded to work on the class members. It was the most beautiful feeling and they looked so relaxed and at peace.

We all went back into the other room and received our certificates. As our Master handed me mine, he stopped. He told the class "I have never spoken in an attunement; I did with Ellen— I welcomed her home.

I drove home with a smile I just couldn't wipe off my face.

∾∾ ∾∾ ∾∾

I waited as long as the Master told me, to go back and do Level Two. This one we can send distant Reiki and work at a higher energy level. We are also qualified practitioners. We can then be paid for our time and energy.

My first few clients I didn't want them to pay me, this job is heart work for me. I quickly learned in my line of work you need some form of payment. So, in comes my first client. As I go to begin, a chime goes six times. We had just laughed that I would not be talking till the end of the session. World peace.

"I'm sorry but did you hear chimes?".

"Yes", she says.

"Okay it's not just me".

She seemed to float away so quick. I tried to wake her, and she would not open her eyes. Oh dear... what have I done? Next thing six chimes again and her eyes open.

It so happens that the house next door use to be the Japanese gardens here a long time ago. I saw my neighbour the next day and asked if she had chimes? I'd never heard them. She replied "oh sorry were you working?, I moved my chimes to clean the area and put them back up".

I smiled and said "perfect timing".

I went on to heal many—my Reiki seemed to take on a life of its own. I started with aromatherapy and Reiki.

Loved my oils.

Not long after I began to be drawn to the amazing power of crystals. So, before I knew it my Reiki guides had me working with those in a healing session as well and every healing was so different.

A few months later I was guided to do a massage course. It was a beautiful day and there I learned; touch is love. So, me being me put it all together with a reading to finish up. Still more. I then added in for you let your soul pick oils of your choice and I use these oils to make you a roller bottle to take home.

Then after a funny experience at work were, I thought an echidna was running around. My boss explained no Ellen, that's a spirit animal. I came home and started seeing or hearing the name of them, so I added them as well.

I left it about a year and my friend Lou was up to doing her Masters.

"Let's do it together", I said. She had a different Master, so I went to meet her—Mumma Bear as we call her. One of the most beautiful angels in human form I had ever met. I knew with that first Mumma Bear hug she was to be my Master.

The day came I was to become master. I was all dressed and excited when Lou came. You get me in spirit, and I light up like a child. I said on the way in, it all just resonates Lou.

She looked at me and said "that's a big word, do you know the meaning?"

Laughing my head off I said "no, but we will soon I bet".

We were met at the door by a huge smile and a Mumma Bear hug. Hello, my baby bears are you ready? It was a very long day. My Master attunements were so different to the others. I sat there and took it all in.

I heard her say "when you are ready open your eyes I'll be behind you". I slowly came back to earth and in front of me was a huge lotus blossom painting I knew I would sit in front of one day. The most incredible thing was I turned to Mumma there was a young lady sitting there. I said "where is Mumma Bear?", she said "I am her. You gifted me back for the attunements with peace love and light".

I love working with Reiki to this day. I've added much to my healings as I've grown. I love to use my crystals still but most of all now–after more study I am doing at present–I love to use imaginary guided healings.

It works like magic.

CHAPTER 13

Shazell Comes to Life

Laying on the lounge one day I hear a voice say, 'if you build it, they will come'. I had a laugh and went to get a cold drink–it was one of the hottest days in years. Again, I hear it. Okay, it's Shaz, I say "it's bloody hot out there", I hear, "you have a cement pond use it as you go". So with that, down I went, a lounge, a table and a statue. I scrubbed and started to order curtains and a tablecloth to set the mood.

I owned three packs of cards at the time, but why not give this a try. I set up a Facebook page and said I was taking bookings. Then before I knew it, I had a few keen to try. I guess I did not believe in my heart this would happen, but it looked like we were off and running with Shazell.

My first client arrived, and I was so scared I don't know how the words were even coming from my mouth. Suddenly, I felt her husband and the rest was history. I was blessed with a very chatty soul here. I was talking, she was crying, and she was smiling and nodding all at once.

He had taken over for me, this was amazing, everything I said she agreed. After a while I pulled my cards out. They validated all I had been saying and gave me some future visions for her, these came to fruition not long after.

See it's easy to sit there and read and channel, it's great to get validations as we go. For a reader the best feeling is when later down the track, they ring or confirm what you had been blessed to tell them.

My greatest gift is finding babies.

I can't even count how many I have found.

I found a very special one nine months ago and can't wait to meet her very soon. My sixth grandchild, a blessing I never believed I would see.

I am sure Cathy went to the big man on this one. She has tested us a few times, this little lady.

∾ ∾ ∾

So, I kept reading away and word got out that I seemed to be blessed with a beautiful gift. It was not long and I was doing up to five readings a day. I did not want money I just wanted to help heal. I never wanted anyone to feel alone and lost like I did when I lost Cathy.

I loved reading in the space I had set up, it didn't take long for it to start filling up with lots of gifts. I would not take money, so the flowers and gifts kept coming. My love of crystals started to build, and the room was being filled with beautiful crystal energy.

I couldn't help but use any excuse to pop over to Reflections Within and look for more crystals. Like a worker can never have enough tools, right? One day as I walked in, Max was on her laptop looking up my Facebook page. She turned and said "oh wow honey I'm just about to message you—how would you like to be a reader at my next fair?"

My head said no... my mouth said yes.

She could see my fear and said "are you ready?".

Again "yes".

Thanks Spirit—we need to be pushed out of our comfort zone at times.

I came home scared as, but it was a dream to read in that room with the other readers. I did not sleep much the night before. When I woke my anxiety was through the roof. I said to Greg "I'll look like a fool–they will be all reading and I'll be just sitting there".

To my shock I was wrong—first reading and I was off! Sitting in a room with a few that had read to me over the years–was little old me, up there right alongside them. Magic happens when you step up to what Spirit knows you can do.

That day I think I got seven readings. Wow I didn't expect that many and Max, with her big smile said "well done".

I nearly drove the car off the road on the way home. I was spirit drunk and so shocked in myself. I did run off the road and nearly hit a pole. Wow I was flying high. I met Greg at a party, and I was driving everyone mad as I just could not come down off this high. Then instantly, a feeling I've learned after fairs and big days—I hit a wall. I left the party, came home and don't remember my head hitting the pillow that night. I know my head was that big it would have hit hard.

I was so happy in myself, the next morning I felt I could fly. A Spirit high is the best. I finally felt this gift was so special to me that I didn't care who judged me—and trust me... we get judged. I'm sure some Sitters, as we call clients at Fairs, come to challenge this gift we are blessed with.

For the first time ever I didn't care. I finally found a place I fit.

Shazell was getting busy I was building a great client base. I would read with the help of my guides and my client's passed loved ones. Before a client appointment one day, I picked up a pen and the words started to flow onto the paper. This was magic! It would show them that Spirit was real and could communicate through me.

I would receive information at times that no one but the client knew. Sometimes it's like putting bits of a puzzle together but in the end that piece of paper I give them to take home is not only validation their loved ones are there–it opens the door to many issues that need to be dealt with for them to live their future free from past hurts. This is where Reiki comes in, they come back and I give them Reiki with all the love and strength in me to clear and balance their energy. It may be done in one healing but most come back for at least four sessions with me. They will then know when they feel they need another one. Some have been coming to me weekly or fortnightly because they love the whole healing I give.

I have added much to my Reiki over time, warm crystals, reflexology guided by Spirit, and I love to give a good head and shoulder massage. Who doesn't love a good massage? so why not throw it in. Touch is love as they say.

I'm about to study reflexology to add to my Reiki.

∾∾ ∾∾ ∾∾

While building a great client base here, one day I got a text of one of my friends in the psychic world. She told me she had given my name to a friend that had a shop close by, and was looking for a reader. Wow was I ready for this? again self-doubt told me no.

I went up and met her and she offered me to work Fridays. I loved the feeling and energy of the shop and working there . I learnt much from my time there but Shazell was my home and I seem to have more bookings here. So, I guess Spirit brought me home.

I started to get feelings in my body and signs to show me how their loved ones had passed over. My main sign was my throat closed over and I would struggle to talk if I had a suicide come in. This was why I was doing this work. I had a beautiful client who had lost her partner and when we met it was still so early and so raw. I received so much information before my client arrived that nobody but these two knew. She was so touched, and I passed on the feelings of the night she had taken herself home.

A long friendship of trust was built with this client—her trust in me was amazing and the information I was given to pass on was so clear.

I have worked with so many families of these lost souls who just could not stay in this lifetime. It has taught me much and helped me with my loss of Cathy. Some tell me they had been wanting it for a long time, others say their mind just snapped and they could not stay.

Even the past weekend I read for two different families. Both showed me once they got to a certain point, it was like it was robotic. They could feel and see what they were doing but couldn't stop the process. One took themselves home by hanging. I said "yes but he could have stopped had he wanted to". She looked at me and said "yes, he could have reached the ground".

Same as Cathy my heart is at peace because I know she could have saved herself. They say this is our book of life–we can't change how we come into it, and how we leave. They all assure me there is no middle place just for suicides. This hurt me so much–someone told me they need to go to be judged. Why would this be when their lives may have been full of pain?

To me my sister was a hero.

She knew we all waited for the call that she had taken herself home for years and, sadly she knew with her mental health issues she was causing us heartache.

CHAPTER 14

My World Changes

Early on the morning of 25 February 2020, I woke to my home phone ringing from my baby girl Cody. Her due date was March 10, although I had said for many months, she would have Macy on February 26, that date was strong in my mind and I was not letting it go. She had a planned C Section booked for March 2 at the time and laughed at me so many times.

Her friend was booked to have her little man that day, so she was determined it wait. I arrived at her place one day and Cody said her friend was in early labour.

I thought, so Cody will get her date as Macy will come early as Grammy said. Still laughing at me Cody said, "no Mum that's too early I can't have her then. So, I think we will see". Macy went quiet so mummy had to have a check over she was tiny, and the doctor said she may be better out to grow more.

He pulled her date forward to the twenty-sixth. I was jumping around so proud I'd won. That soon changed. At 4.30am on February 25 I could hear my phone ringing. I fell over the bed screaming "oh my God it's Cody!"

Sure, enough it was, so calm she said "my waters have broken and I'll head into the hospital at six to see what they will do". She talked to Greg and we were all so calm. I was not happy till she was safe at the hospital mind you. She told me the doctor would be in at 8.00am to check her and come back after his morning clients to deliver her. My words were "well I'm telling you, she will not wait and be there by nine."

So, I'm walking around the house in circles so excited and scared all at once. I feel in my head get ready she will be here soon. My friend Amanda rang me as I had accidently called her, and I chatted for a bit. She is very gifted as well and at the same time we said "I must go... that baby is here." Sure, enough I text Corey and said "she is here I can feel it."

Sure, enough he sent me a picture of my tiny dancer holding her tiny dancer on her heart. My poor dog I screamed so loud he bolted.

Macy Catherine Clare was here, a tiny little five-pound five divine little fairy had entered our world. The love I felt when I saw her, and her Mummy was a feeling I wish I could bottle. I stood there and looked at my baby with hers and the tears were in my eyes. When Cody handed me this tiny little old soul my heart overflowed with a love only a grandmother knows.

Her eye opened and looked at me like, okay you're that voice I've heard so much. I took my Mum in the next day and that room should have exploded with the love within those walls. Cody got gold stars as a new mummy and took dolly as I call her home early. Home to become a little family. I was just so happy the world was perfect.

CHAPTER 15

The World is put on Hold—Covid-19

I have been wanting to get on and put my feelings down for a few weeks but to be truthful I've been lost. The world is lost, and my words were lost. New words run our world now due to a virus that will never be forgotten. COVID-19 locked our world down. My OCD anxiety went into overdrive. Every day new rules and new words. social distancing, lockdown, stay safe stay home.

We are not allowed to see family; we are not allowed to leave our house unless it's for work or to get essential needs. I don't go into the shops. Greg does as it's safer just one of us goes. I did go in last week and it's so scary. Tape on the floor showing how to stay a safe distance at the checkout, tap and go, no money, no virus spread.

We can walk which has become my sanity, although we mustn't sit in a park or bench while out. We are not allowed to have anyone visit our house. This is so hard with my grandchildren, especially a brand new baby girl. I can't go and see my Mummy as she has a low immune system due to cancer. I felt like my world was over.

I had to do my job still and I felt my Shazell team needed me more than ever. I wanted so badly to get on with life but I was grieving my life that was taken so quickly. I had to feel this and try healing it first. So, I meditated and prayed and gathered my strength to get on and share what I was feeling every day and what they all wanted to ask.

Spirit started to show me many signs and I stared to lift. I meditated on a sign we would all be okay. I was shown a black and white feather. That day we went for our walk I had to do a quick side-track. As I looked down each side of my show was one white feather and one black. The next day a close friend who lost her mother only the week before woke to a white feather on her table. She said is this from Mum. It sure was but she was giving more than my friend a message here.

We were out walking one day, and decided to walk past Mum's. I rang her and said come out the front. The look on her face was priceless. We air hugged and stayed our distance. As I write this, I can't wait to hug her and not let her go. I have good days but then I can go into huge lows. I want to hold all my kids and their kids. I feel so much for so many who have lost their jobs, I'm trying so hard to hold everyone up in the background as our fears are real.

Some days I want to scream and cry for the world, not for me. I feel safe and I know this will be a new beginning for this earth. Many lessons will be learned and bloody hard ones for sure. I have my own theories on what's happening here and had spoken about it before it happened. That will not change this now but it's day by day with no idea of the end of this nightmare.

As I write it's April 5 and my guides and feelings tell me we will lift in May. I feel an Australian will find a very simple cure and this will go as quick as it came. They say it started in China and that's where the world heart chakra is said to be. Maybe she is open waiting to be healed. I have many visions in my meditations–there is a grey cloud over the earth. There will be purple rain and we will dance and hug in the streets again.

It will take the world a long time to get over this, I see maybe years before being able to travel internationally. The stocks will rise, and we will rise. I believe we learn to live much more off our own country's products.

Sadly, Australians were shown all over the world as heroes in our dealing of the fires and drought. When this virus hit, we were shown as mad people fighting over toilet rolls. Why the toilet roll? I still don't get, and you still need to be lucky to get your hands on some. Sitting on the toilet one day I thought soon not only will we sit in peace; we will shit in peace knowing we can get toilet rolls again.

Facebook and the media are having a field day slamming many world leaders and praising others. I would hate to be our Prime Minister now. I don't follow politics but wow he's had a lot to deal with from the beginning of this year. Everyone begging for lockdown, he's trying to leave as many as he can out there for the economy, but wow these rules do not add up. For me, I just went into 'home is safe, stay there'. Sadly many still ran to the beach and shopping centres, so now we have the privilege of a drive or a family visit taken away.

I am actually getting things done I did not have time to do. I finished my Holistic counselling course and came through with two distinctions–that shocked the hell out of me, I must say.

So, it has now May 9, I have been online every day trying to hold everyone together in this new crazy way to live. The curve, safe places, social distancing, CV-19 shut the world down. I am still walking each day and I must say my curves are leaving me. I have lost 12 kilos and keeping my body fit against any illness.

Last week they lifted the rules to have two adults and their children to your home. Bless be me—all my grandchildren back having a sleep over. To hug them was just magic.

May 1 we got our first freedom and it will be a three-stage process.

The words, spike and second wave are worldwide as many countries are opening. One of the biggest questions is the bloody pub—got to love Australia. I must say I am sitting waiting on shops and motels to be open to run away with Cody and magic Macy as I call her. This little poppet lights my heart up. I am really missing Shazell, but it seems spirit had a huge healing for me in this lockdown.

I was happy doing some online readings and as I said doing my live readings to keep us all okay. Coming to the end of my counselling course, out of nowhere came a huge flash back of my life at about the age of fourteen. A text from a friend and study just lined up and dropped me. I vomited and sat there like I was out of my body watching it all. The man in the mask was back.

This was all new to me. My councillor said it is normal to block and not see a trauma like this. I do not want to go into detail here but wow it set the healer back a few pegs. I put on my mask and did as I teach. Feel. Deal. Heal. I felt free from it all at last.

∾∾ ∾∾ ∾∾

The peace was not to last. The second Covid wave they were waiting for–hit me big time. My beautiful friend Amanda asked me to do a healing on a very eccentric man we call Bobby D. It was a Sunday and I don't work Sundays That soon changed as the pain I was getting was spot on with him. A beautiful lady in spirit called Jeannie came in singing.

She used to sing with him as he played the organ. His music is magic and for a man of ninety, all I can say is wow! I told him to lay down and I would send distant healing. Halfway through I stopped and told Amanda has he been resuscitated a few times. Also I could not feel his toes–like frost bite. All were validated and much more. He had been so bad and never felt that way, so he was down for the count.

That night he rang Amanda and said "who is this crazy lady? I am flying!". It was the strangest night like we were all spirit drunk. He had not been sleeping but had a great night's sleep. He had rung to thank me in person, but I had passed out.

The next day he rang me full of so much excitement. I was stumped–for the first time in my life I couldn't get a word in.

He had so much to share with me, he said "okay hang on I am going cross eyed Ellen". Holding on the other end of the phone, I was thinking, shit is he okay. I later learned this was his way of telling me he was about to read me. You see he goes off and talks to his clairvoyants. I was speechless to hear him telling me so much of my life. So many things I had been doing this very week.

∾ ∾ ∾

A pandemic that stopped the whole world and an eccentric amazing man gave me all the time and information I needed to see Ellen. This is when the name of my book changed again. As the journey of an author continues, so does the title of the book. This week my book's name is 'The Healer Within Me'.

There I was, as Bobby D put it—the little girl with the back-the-front life. Healed some more, ready to heal and be there for many.

∾∾ ∾∾ ∾∾

In the middle of all this meeting him and the world spinning I felt myself going back down the dark rabbit hole. It seems I had to go back and see and deal with a few things in my past I had blocked from my mind.

It's so strange as this was a huge thing to take in. Yet after many tears I felt myself climbing back up that bloody dark hole and back out into my magic one. As I sit and write, I feel free and determined to live the rest of my life to the fullest. A lot of things happened in my childhood. So, the rest is mine. I choose to heal and stay in my magic while I travel and live my life.

Bobby D gave us quite the scare. He loves swimming to keep his body 'well oiled'. With Covid-19 sadly the Bondi pool closed along with the rest of the world. We are slowly opening things up and being given a chance at freedom. Every country, every state is opening with different rules. I must say none of the rules of this whole pandemic have ever added up.

For Bobby D, his pool opening was a huge leap to freedom. With towel in hand and his huge smile he hobbled into the pool. Only to be told at the gate "no sorry your ten minutes late for your half hour, you can't go in.

Now our man of many words tried his magic, showing them his feet and saying it was so hard to get there and to please let him in, but was told no. So, home he went still not feeling well and feeling very let down. He had worked tirelessly over the weekend before on some new music. Mind you I had listened to it and it was pure magic. Please feel free to look him up on YouTube and be drawn in by this magic music. Robert Goode, I just get lost in his music and his talent. How he did this last lot amazes me, well I do know him, I know many spirits would have been helping his hands and feet as what he did was near impossible.

So, the next day full of excitement he arrived at the pool. To our horror he had a massive heart attack in there. The fear I feel he felt was terrifying. He was rushed to hospital by ambulance. I had been telling Amanda I saw him going there by ambulance and his medication needing to be sorted.

Bobby had so many more episodes he scared the hell out of all of us. It was a long day, so I took myself to bed and kept sending all the healing I had in me to him. The next day he was sitting up reading all the staff and the doctors he could fit in that room. I believe this man had the one and only Victor Chang massaging his heart in that pool that day.

He is doing so much better every day. His medications have been all sorted and I hope he's home in a few days. I know there is a reason he was sent to my life–he closed my circle– and I am blessed. I feel I was sent to his life, as some of the work I have done on him and the feedback he gives me, is nothing short of miraculous.

CHAPTER 16

Covid Slows while the World Hurts

At last! good news–many restrictions are now easing—it feels so good to go and do the things we took for granted before lockdown. Just to see people sitting in a park having a picnic, go out for tea. There are still some restrictions in place but it feels so good after the last few months.

Sadly today I go to a funeral of a very loved man–and the restrictions limit us to fifty people. In saying this I know many who have passed over the last few months and it was only ten people who could attend.

There have been many lessons learned through this time. I continued to work online; and so many marriages broke up, so many people lost themselves, so many people found themselves. Me being one of them.

The last few months dropped me back into some dark places. Yet today I can say it healed me so much. You see I thought I was there on my healing platform, but this time it gave me time to find things in me that still needed to be healed. Today I feel free.

It seems the world is fighting for freedom.

I was hoping to see this as a new world order and healing. Sadly... not so.

Watching television the world is angry and standing by the treatment of coloured people, there are riots and protest all over the world. Finally, we will all come together and stand as one but I guess out of this there is still more healing to be done. I pray for peace every day.

CHAPTER 17

Back to my Magic Carpet Ride

Word got out and I cannot believe to this day where we ended up. With Reiki it was a nice balance as I would read for them then work with Reiki to heal. Life was like living a dream. As I went on, I found so many beautiful friends through clients. Every day I would shock myself with the validation I would get.

It can be so sad, so deep, and so hard for me in there as most the things I am healing in people I have lived. It gives me that special connection with them as I know what they are really feeling, so I give it my heart and soul.

I love working with children, they call me Fairy El and I call it fairy tickles. The most amazing thing is when I work with star children—or those born with my gift. To be able to talk to me openly about the feelings and things they see, is just magic. My biggest stand out children would have to be my little spinners.

At a Fair I met three beautiful souls who have become a big part of my heart and my life. Standing there on my first meeting I felt like I was spinning.

I looked at their Mum and said, "I feel like I am spinning." She laughed and said "that's my girls". So, booking a reading with me I said to her "I feel like I can see a Russian doll spinning". She replied that's little A, as I call them, she dances and spins round and round.

So, the time came for her reading and yep, the room was spinning, these girls are all magic, so the world does spin with them. The reading went well, and the mother was keen to have some well needed Reiki to ground her. That weekend I went to a psychic fair, I was not working so it was good to sit back and take in the magic. My teacher was doing platform. I sat at the back so Shaz would not gate crash the reading, as she always does when she gets up.

I looked up and my teacher was swaying and looking around lost, I pointed down to the girls before she started and caught the mother's eye. I said honey move the girls and the feeling of spinning stopped. These girls had some crazy spirit energy.

Finally, the day came they were at Shazell for some Reiki. Wow the whole room was spinning I think I fell a few times. Little A started talking to spirit straight away and let us just say she loves the floor. She will be on stage for sure all her life. Big A got up to go first and we connected heads straight away. I felt Shaz standing beside me, I said "you see someone beside me can't you honey?". Her eyes lit up, "yes", she said and continued to tell me what she had on and described her perfectly.

This was the start of many fun adventures in Spirit for all of us. When she got in the car, she was busting with excitement that I, not only believed her, I knew what she could see. We would play guessing games and both girls would get the questions correct most times. I would give them homework, they loved it. The most important job was I balanced them. Little A set me the task, with lots of love and tender care, lots of tears—we got there after a few visits.

One day was so magical, they had been away, and big A had got terribly upset on her way home. She told me she thought a circus had burned down there. Well, this set off a huge few hour. I fell into channelling and could see the circus acts. The girls were validating all I said and felt they had been in that circus. Mother spinner was sitting in the corner on Google, we even got the name of the circus and a date in the eighteen hundred or there about.

So many days so many stories have been had with these girls. When I was going to America, they were so excited as I wanted to go to Disneyland and meet Micky Mouse. Little A said with excitement you are I see you in black tights in front of the castle. I did not get there but I was standing in front of Hurst Castle. They amazed me and still do. I had to tell them sadly as a star child we get judged, and to be mindful who they talked to about Spirit as the world doesn't see through our eyes.

I wish I hadn't listened to all the people who told me to turn my gift off so many years ago. If I know these girls, they will stand strong in their gift young, and shine. If you are reading this my little fairies shine bright and never let anyone dull your magic.

CHAPTER 18

Never a dull Moment

Some days when I am working in Shazell I think my neighbours must think I'm mad. They all know my job and how deep it must be. Yet all you hear most days is laughing, I do not like my clients to leave sad and somehow can turn sad into mad. So many come and go I cannot ever remember faces or what I have read. Just the other day I finally got to do face to face after they lifted Covid rules.

A beautiful client came in, as she sat, I thought, please calm down darling, I told her I was there to help her to feel better, lots of tears later I was teaching her to feel go deep and heal. I said if it gets to deep think of a happy time please. Still crying I got up to get her something, as I walked back, I fell. We'll let us just say I nearly landed in her rabbit hole. She burst out laughing saying oh I am so sorry I always laugh when people fall over. Tears coming out of my eyes from laughing I said oh let me tell you that is me.

The rest of the reading was so funny, and she left a vastly different lady to who walked in. The next morning she messaged me... she felt the best she had felt in years. She then said is it okay that every time I am sad, I think of your face while falling and laugh. I lost it. My job was done.

So many life changing healing continued in there, as I was healing them words would come out of my mouth and those would stick in my mind that I needed on my healing journey. A friend I had not seen for a long time came to me one day. This friend to me was an incredibly beautiful looking head-strong lady. She had sadly lost her father and with him so much of that strength left her as well.

I would be laying here and get an urge to text her–she wore a good mask and said she was fine all the time–bless her. A marriage break up and a gym accident changed her life again for the worst. I text again and she started to let me chip the mask away. Trust meant so much to this poor broken soul. I finally talked her into coming to Shazell, she was broken like I have never seen anyone before. My heart broke for her and this was to be my biggest turn around ever. My mind was thinking where do I start? what do I do?

That is when Spirit stepped in and took my hand, heart and soul to guide me. I had to separate my feelings here or I would breakdown with her. Her Dad came in spirit and stated to share things only she knew–bless him–as this gained her trust, he would give me stories to make her smile... that huge smile she is well known for again.

After a few visits we tried Reiki for her back. It was just too painful for her to lay or sit there in a chair. She was one tough cookie as I get a bit of the pain they feel as an energy collector and there was not much of her mind, body and soul that was not broken.

It blew me away how hard she went, in the trust she gave me. Her Dad was there all along, but I soon felt another energy come in and start to give me messages. I went to meet her beautiful dog one day and have a nice cuppa and chat. Her smile was back, and it made my heart sing.

As I hugged her goodbye that day, I felt this new energy again. I said wow sis you're going to be riding a new bike with a man very soon. She grabbed me and laughed and off I drove. I did not hear from her for a few weeks, so I texted "come on sis he's here I bet". Sure, enough he was and did ride a bike.

All Spirit had showed me here was like a fairy tale, I remember thinking oh come on, yet I had shared all this with her weeks before. So, it seems the new spirit energy was this man's father who had been working some magic in the spirit world for this pair.

All I had shared came true. Magic really happens when you believe. They married and they both live happy ever after.

CHAPTER 19

The Bay Getaway

I feel it's fitting that I am at my favourite place as a child with Cathy, with my daughter and her magic little lady Macy Catherine. So much has changed in our world over the past six months with Covid-19. It's so nice to be able to get away after lockdown as it's called. The talk of a second wave is very scary. Sadly, Victoria is in stage four lockdown.

It's so hard to watch them going through this again. The suicide rate from the first lockdown was so big. The fear and job losses are just too much for the human mind. This is such an unknown journey the world is living. The virus seems to spin its web very quick. So many different opinions, I find the best thing is to keep my opinion to myself. I trust and pray by September it will leave as quick as it came. The new fashion and safe way when out is the highly unfashionable face mask. I still feel safe to travel as much as it scares my poor mother.

There have been hot spots at Salamander Bay close by to where we are. This was several weeks ago but and they go in and clean very quickly now. This is our life for now, so I go away when I can, as you just don't know if we will be put back into lockdown. So, as they say "let's play while the sun shines".

I sit here with the sun shining through the window watching Macy bouncing in her jolly jumper with squeals of delight. I think what this world is going to be like for this little magic fairy. She brings out the magic in me. Each day a new day full of so much to learn and so much to see.

Cody actually blessed me with this trip for some time out. The past few months have really set the level of learning for me. After my breakdown life kept throwing so many more lessons my way. Sometimes it feels like I am being tested by Spirit. It's crazy as after each lesson I make it through to say, my reading connection is so much stronger.

There have been so many universal tests this year with four retrogrades in a row, on top of the uncertainty and negative energy out there. Being an energy collector and an empath, I must stay protected as much as I can. I try to shine a positive on lives on Shazell as much as I can without giving too much opinion. Like I said there are so many views on this virus.

I wish the whole world could sit together in peace at the same time and throw nothing but positive energy as it's so hard to see it for many. Life is just so different, so many out there that cannot see their own family and do not know when. Some say no world travel for four years now. Even here we can't cross the borders at the moment. What is this virus that has separated the world? I pray for a vaccine every night so we can live the life we knew.

Sadly, when we were given some freedom into the world, so much anger came from the people. To watch the news would bring me to tears. Our world seems as sick as the virus, you cannot help but pick up on the negativity and the fear.

All my beautiful spirit healer friends have been tested like me. Mind body and soul deep. Many like me doubting or trying to run from this beautiful gift with were blessed with, instead of embracing it. I wanted to close my gift so bad the other month, when a trip to Byron Bay for my husband's sixtieth turned to shit.

It seems I picked up a lost soul. She was full of sorrow and I could not understand why I just wanted to sit and cry. I was shown she was stuck here from the 1890s. I was feeling all the pain of her passing, so much so I thought I was having a heart attack. It did not hit me what it was till I got home and meditated.

I set her free. It felt awesome after all those years to walk her to the light and to the bridge–many souls show me after they pass.

So as rewarding as my beautiful gift is, it can throw me some huge curve balls. I came home wanting to run from my gift as I get so tired with this work. I had been shown once again Spirit does not know holidays, bless. The energy I use just in a day out –if I am not protected–can be so draining. Not to say when I do five healings a day. I find I need lots more time off to make sure I do not run myself into the ground. The emotions in one day can be so high, then so low I want to sit and cry. Every time I feel like giving in, I think of how beautiful my heart feels when someone sends me a message saying how much better they feel. Or as I love most how they are pregnant after many years of trying. Let me say I have known many babies are there before anyone else does.

I get lots of text messages with a picture of a positive pregnancy test. So if you don't want to know, do not come to the baby finder. The best one I ever got was from my daughter this time last year. How my phone screen did not smash I will never know.

We have returned from the Bay and I have just had an online interview about my book with a beautiful lady who popped into my life just when I needed her. I honestly said I do not even know where to begin writing it and how. Well, here I am and loving the healing I have received from writing.

CHAPTER 20

Dean makes his Entrance

One night just as I was falling asleep, I saw and felt a very real sensation. I sat up to make sure it was not a dream. I saw like long green and blue orbs floating around my room. Next as clear as anything I could see a crochet bedspread. I had a strong feeling I had seen this before but could not put together where.

It woke me up, so I sat up and jumped on Facebook to kill some time reading. As I scrolled through, I came upon a picture on my friend's page. I cannot remember if it was the bedspread or what it was, but I knew this was it. I remember my friend saying her brother had stage four cancer. This was who it was contacting me.

I looked at the time and it was late so I thought, I will text her in the morning. To my surprise she beat me too it. She texted and said "my brother Dean needs you Ellen". Now this one did surprise me. I explained to my friend what had happened, and she was not surprised at all.

So that week I went to meet him. He was out the back sitting in his throne as I like to call it. He would sit out there for hours, even through the night. You see he loved his smokes and was not giving them up I learned quickly. His sisters would sit beside him, too scared to leave his side.

They did not want to lose their baby brother. His beautiful wife beside him looked up with pain in her eyes, she was so tiny and so tired bless her. He told me she was his princess and that she was.

With a big gulp and trust in myself I could do this I asked Dean and her to come inside. He wanted Reiki but he wanted to ask me what it was going to be like when his time came. This big gentle giant was so scared it nearly broke me. Gathering my strength and looking into their eyes as they held hands, I told them all I have been shown through Spirit.

He got very agitated–the fear of the unknown was too much for him. He grabbed his wife and said "how can I leave her", looking out at his family he said "and those girls". I calmed him the best I could and asked if he would like Reiki–I was going to be there to help him to the end. Holding hands, I said to her "you will feel this as well honey and you need this". Reiki can travel long distances; the blessing is if you are in the same room you will also receive a healing.

Laying his trust in me I held his head and commenced our first Reiki session. I did not know what this gentle giant would feel. I gave him all I had in me and felt an instant acceptance. I worked on him from head to toe. I then worked on them as a pair and joined their hands in healing. He sat up and I could not believe my eyes. He looked so much younger and said he was feeling so much better. We were all so shocked at the change in him.

He walked out the back to his sisters and they were as shocked as us. He was chatty as and I then met the very cheeky Dean. We all sat and laughed and talked for so long. I pulled some cards for all that were there. They all loved their messages from passed loved ones.

The next time I arrived he had all his mates there, he stood and said this is Ellen we will be back. We went inside and I said "Dean they have come to see you, as some were coming to say goodbye and time was precious", he replied "and you have come to give me Reiki".

We were halfway through and he kept saying the same thing over and over., I thought he said the fridge, and he kept saying "… all the colours, oh they're so pretty". They had upped his meds and I thought I'll have what he's having. Then he said "Ellen I cannot leave the girls yet".

When we finished, we sat inside alone, just him and his wife and me. He looked like he was so at peace. He said the bridge is everything you showed me, as he shared, he was so full of peace, he kept saying the colours over and over. To see such a big man melt was so incredible.

We would sit and talk after each healing; he was a character that's for sure. One day we figured out we actually went to the same schools since we were so young. He always had his bit of a story to tell all who were there after I healed him. It was so good to see him light up.

The thing that touched me so much was all his mates would be there and he would openly speak of what he has seen and my gift. Many judge and do not believe my gift. This man sure did and he wanted to share it to anyone that listened.

The last few times I arrived he would be asleep; he was slipping away each week. I did a healing as he slept the whole time. When he woke, he went mad on his wife and I as this was his weekly treat. He got up and shocked them all as he had been in bed most days now. He went to his throne and all his girls sat by his side.

I felt blessed to be there in these final days that were so precious to them all. He asked me what made me a Reiki master.

I said "to me it's just a higher level of practitioner". I also said "I do not take the label master as there are many over me, I respect and call that". His reply was "but you are a master at what you do".

As I said goodbye that day, I knew I would not see him again, I said take care I will see you soon and wanted to cry. He looked at me and said "goodbye master Ellen". I made it to the car and sat with tears in my eyes. I knew my job there was done, I just had to stay connected and get him home peacefully with distant Reiki.

He was not with us much longer, his wish to was pass at home, but it got too hard to control his pain. He went to hospital while the girls sat all day and some nights with him, bless them. They really upped his medication one day. As I worked, I heard him saying, "wow this is good stuff, I am not leaving here while I have this".

His sister came and rang me, her words were "he's loving these drugs and no pain, he's not going anywhere". I laughed and said "he just told me that". He showed me signs to the end that she would ring and validate.

He finally put on his white and gold coat and set out on his journey to the bridge he had seen in our Reiki session months before. His wife and son beside him and his sisters sleeping in the hospital lounge. A few days after his funeral I saw him dancing in white pants and a white top.

∽∽ ∽∽ ∽∽

The girls came for Reiki that Friday and I showed them how he was dancing. Tears rolling down my friend's face, she said "that's how he danced Ellen".

I am sure he is still up there dancing and looking down on them all.

Dean, I thank you for sharing your end days with me. I thank you for your trust and I thank you for seeing me as a master of what my heart work is.

CHAPTER 21

Stepping up to the Stage

Over the years I use to watch John Edwards and so many do what I call platforming. I was blown away by their ability to connect with Spirit at their shows. So many people, so many souls wanting to come through and give messages to their loved ones. Funny thing was I was watching a friend I had made at Reflection Within when I was again told to embrace my gift. I went to sit at the front so she would see me and pick me. I heard my head say *'if it's meant to be Spirit will find you'*.

I then went and sat in the back row. First up I see her walking towards me. She looks at me and says "you need to fix your stomach problems you have and start working in Spirit". She delivered so many things that were spot on. I looked in her eyes and she was so scared. She was not a fan of the stage as amazing as she was. To this day I still thank her for pushing me to my gift. It was time.

I have already shared, I had done some fairs and definitely found my place and my magic. Fair days are so amazing. I just light up and feel like I am flying. To be sitting in that room with so many talented readers that I have sat for is mind blowing.

The excitement and spirit in the room needs to be bottled. I was feeling confident and dropping my fear at last after about three fairs. The text I love arrived... 'Ellen can you read at this fair?'. I quickly replied 'yes'. Next thing I get another text 'good! will you platform?'. Oh, my I must be honest–I was not confident enough. I know Max would not ask if she didn't think I could do this, but my over thinking killed the moment.

One... I had weight on, and I did not feel confident about standing on a stage with everyone looking at me. Next, I did not trust Spirit would back me and, my biggest mistake... I did not trust myself. She gave me a day to think about it. I chickened out big time.

This worked out in the favour of a client I taught by now, not that she needed it. I sent her home and shared a picture of Shaz with her. She came back a week later, told me things even I did not know about Shaz. Then did a reading for me. She blew me away big time.

She calls me Mum as in her Spirit Mum. She said "okay when will we do our next class?", I laughed and said "honey you do not need a teacher, will you read at a fair I am holding in a month". Cool, sure will - was her reply, she has never been afraid and trusted her guide to back her from day dot. I said to her one day, "baby who is your guide?", she looked at me and said, "Shaz of course".

So, after I had knocked back my chance to take the stage, I get an extremely excited phone call, she was going to take the stage.

The day arrived and yes, she was scared, it is so daunting to know you are going up there. I took the hour off to watch her. She was so ready for this. Her mother had never seen her work and I noticed her sitting there. Like two proud Mumma bears we sat and held our breath while she looked for the owner of the first message from the other side.

It is so hard as everyone wants to own them, then wow she

connected so well it blew me away. She walked off the stage to the family and it was like she was reading a book. After this she was on a roll, she knocked it out of the park.

I turned to look and hug her mum and the tears of pride were rolling down her face. She kept saying, I knew she was gifted, never did I know this well. Her mum from that day on has never missed any of us girls on stage.

She left the stage and out of site we hugged and jumped around like kids in a lolly shop. She said "Mum I cannot put into words the high I am on right now. All of me wanted to feel this, yet my fear was just too huge".

With lots of the different kind of Spirits in me, you could not get me off the stage, drink makes us think we sound amazing, also loose the fear of people looking at my body on stage. I went home that night so happy I had been booked out in the reading room, yet I knew a part of me was still waiting.

So, the next fair came, and I got the message, would I like to read and was so excited to say "yes!". She left it till a couple of weeks before the Fair, so I did not stress–and there it was. 'Will you platform?' Before I had time to think I said yes. I was so scared, but I had to do this as part of my life journey.

The next few weeks were so scary, as a huge over-thinker I kept thinking. I have made such a good name for Shazell, what if I fail, what if I faint, what if I fall over up there, what if Spirit does not back me?

So wrong... as I have now learnt and taught. I had the key; it was there–I just needed to accept Ellen and never doubt Spirit has my back again.

∾ ∾ ∾

As I stood and looked out into the audience all I could see was so many pairs of eyes, begging me to pick them. I had sat there so many times praying for the same. Funny to think it was someone giving me a message at a fair just like this.

I had been getting a message from a little boy who said, find my mummy since the night Max asked me to platform. He said I have two teddy bears not one two, one is incredibly special to her. You will find her if you trust me.

So, okay there I was. I was scared and frozen then I just opened my mouth, and I could hear myself saying these words. To my horror no one out there hands go up or seem to connect. Not the way to start, let me tell you. Suddenly, I saw a huge smile and heard, that is for me. Turns out she was a reader in the room with me and walked in a little late.

From there on it just flowed, I walked off stage and down to each person I had a special message for that day. As my nerves calmed, I got playful as it can be so deep giving or as I know receiving at a platform event. So much validation came through it blew me away.

I will never forget the magic I felt alive in me as I walked from the room that day. I do not think my head or feet landed for days. I did it!, I faced my fears, as my master has taught me before I walked up there. What is fear Ellen? I said me laughing, she said "no, fear is fear of fear itself. Yet if you are scared and you beat it Ellen you become a hero to yourself.

This was the beginning of a magic carpet ride for me, I never want to get off. Shazell just kept getting bigger and bigger. I loved mixing my readings with Reiki as it seemed to bring balance to my day. I started to do some guided meditation for them as I shared my Reiki to give them a touch more healing.

I would go to bed of a night and wake to another idea I could use. All my life I would put a plan together and start but not finish. Not this time I want it to grow and heal as many as I can reach. As to why I am writing this book.

My life to many may have something in it that resonates with their life. To show we are not alone is my biggest wish even if it means showing parts of my life many would not share.

CHAPTER 22

Pocket Rocket

At many of the fairs I had been to and worked, I kept running in to this amazing little ball of energy I like to call, pocket rocket. Sheb is a world of knowledge who has so much to share in life, sometimes I wait for her to combust through her smile.

One day she texted and asked me for a reading. I must say I was nervous as she was super woman to me. I had learned relaxation massage from her in a fun workshop and did pick up a lot of her energy and past loved ones that day.

She arrived with that smile that could light up the world and the connection was crazy. We laughed, we cried. Most of all what I saw in her future was huge. This little energy will go far. Watch this space as when they open the world, she will work all around it.

A beautiful friendship started that day, I am forever grateful for whoever sent her onto my yellow brick road of magic as she not only taught me so much. She trusted in me more than I did myself back then.

She rang me one day and said , "Ellen can you help me with a workshop I am doing soon?". Excited I said "of course" thinking a quick Reiki or something. She said "I want you to tell your story— I want you to be the other speaker". I was blown away as I had heard Sheb on stage many times and she has so many diplomas under her hat.

Public speaking and fine tuning those skills with Toastmasters she knew her work well. So, without fear this time I said I would be so happy to join you—I can't wait. We did a live to get it out there, with that the bookings came in and we were both so excited to share our knowledge.

We organised to meet at the Yoga Hut for a coffee and a run over what we had planned. Sheb comes rushing in and sits down and proceeds to pull out her folder with all the power points she wants to work through, time slots, everything worked out to the minute. She then looks and says, so where are your notes. I laughed and said "oh I will be okay, spirit has my back it will all come together on the day".

The day arrived and I turned up on what I call my spirit high, the energy in the pictures I take before a fair or workshop seems to glow through my eyes. Strange how the mind thinks as there was no stage, I was on their level and I was not the least bit nervous.

I arrived early in true Ellen style, so I went in and started to set up. Now my carrot cake has been known to fill a party before so I had been teasing all my clients that had tried it that it would be there. I had lots of nice food for our half time break.

The lady who owns it took me to the kitchen and showed me around also what I could use and where the fridge was. Well trying to take it all in and get this show on the road, I put the food in the freezer.

I set up the most magic atmosphere. The magic in the yoga hut just flows, it's a beautiful old church with floors I worship they're so amazing!

When I walk on them, I ground myself on them like the floor

of mother earth herself. Sheb was going over her notes and the energy was building.

Four hours seems so long to get everyone to sit and keep their attention, yet as we opened the doors they came in as excited as we were, bless them. They all took their spots and Sheb let the magic begin. She has a magic way of bringing them all together, they all got to share who they were and what they thought of each other with the person next to them.

I sat and watched her capture them with her magic and wisdom she had been learning all her life. Before I knew it, she was giving me the nod to go and prepare the food. So, I very quietly left the room as they were all transfixed on her.

I went to the fridge as I thought and pulled my carrot cake out and looked with pride. Home made with love. As I put the knife in it was as hard as a rock. Oh, crumbs what have I done. I ran and got the cheeses and meat and sure enough I hit the cabanossi on the bench and it was also frozen solid.

I thought Lou is just there at the door she will know what to do. Next thing I felt what I thought was her behind me. So out loud I said oh shit I frozen the bloody food, help. I turned to see she was not there. I was sure she said calm down put it out on the bench and the sun out there will melt it.

I opened the door and slid down to Lou on floor level. I could not stop laughing. I said I froze the food help. She looked at me although she was transfixed on Sheb. Again, laughing so hard I was in a ball I opened the door and said help.

Sheb heard me and said, excuse me Ellen is everything okay out there. I fell out into the room laughing and said, no Huston we have a little problem. I may have frozen the food. The whole room cracked up. Me being me said keep talking for an hour. She looks at me like "okay how?".

"It's okay I've got this," I said.

We finally set it up and it was all just fine. So, as I teach, everything can be fixed. Sheb came to the kitchen and said "here is the fridge honey, that is the freezer".

When we retuned, it was my time to shine. I had no idea what I was going to say or do I just do the same as I was taught to do in my readings. Something I had practiced a little too hard all my life. Talk... let it flow, I started to tell my life journey from waking and knowing they were taking my Daddy forever. I touched on a few deep moments of my life and I looked at a beautiful old man stroking his wife's hand with tears in their eyes. I was not up here to bring them down so I moved forward and took them on my roller coaster ride that is my life.

So many examples I had used in Shazell were used, my fairy tale of getting out of the rabbit hole and finding the magic on the yellow brick road was unfolding without me even thinking what I was doing or saying.

I could see they were all taking it in laughing with me and crying with me. I like to bring them into my excitement and emotions to show them how they hold it all within. I had asked them all as I started to talk, "if I was to give you a magic key right now to control your life, set you free and own that key would you buy it?". The answer was a big room full of hands up.

After I finished what felt like five minutes up there, I said okay, now it is that easy. You hold the key you see; it was there all along; you just need to own it. Sheb was giving me the nod to finish. All of a sudden though I asked them all to bow their heads and lead them in a meditation. Okay this is new guides... let's go. I closed my eyes and I will never forget that moment, I opened my eyes and they were all there with their heads bowed and a smile on their faces.

The biggest smile of all was Sheb at the back of the room. With a huge thumbs up and mouthing, what the hell?. I knew

I did well to get the thumbs up from her. She had unlocked something in me I never knew I could do, bless her. The trust she gave me this day will remain in my heart forever, seems she saw some magic I was yet to bring to life.

Thank you with all my heart Sheb, may you be blessed with a life full of magic and love. I will never forget your love and trust, yet to top it off you get another diploma to add to your magic. You learn hypnotherapy. Again, you ask me to come and be blessed as you are learning.

Well, this was one of the most beautiful healings I have ever had. I will never forget her voice; it was so angelic. I felt so much trust so quickly with her. This is not easy for me, after so many have broken that trust that I loved. We worked with my weight yet as I left, I felt a huge weight full from me.

For once in my life, I did not focus on my food, I just started to eat foods that were good for me and move more. Before I knew it, I was sending her a picture of me down eleven kilos. She had set me free. I was flying.

CHAPTER 23

Crazy Covid

A lot of my weight loss was in the beginning of Covid-19. Thinking back how scared I was now, it kept me going. It was like I had to get out and walk or I would go crazy.

As I write tonight Covid-19 has swept its way around the world. We are still only allowed to travel within Australia and I wonder if we will ever be able to travel this world again.

All our borders opened and it was so emotional watching families meet at the airports. The things we take for granted have definitely been a lesson. As soon as Queensland opened, I got to go for a week with my girls Cody and baby Macy on yet another get away.

As soon as we came out of lock down you could not keep me home. Cody is off on maternity leave and we have made the most of it, that's for sure. Sadly, right on Christmas some new cases emerged in the Northern Beaches in Sydney. Just when it was all starting to look like our new normal.

We still have rules to follow, social distance and hand wash are a part of every day. Restaurants were finally allowing enough people in them for lots to open. They even started live music and the last few weeks we could stand and talk while out, then the best we could dance. This did not last long, yet showed us what we had been missing.

Greg and I actually went to Darling Harbour to stay just before this new outbreak. It was heartbreaking as at home it felt normal yet here so many restaurants were closed. The ones we always loved to sit and enjoy the views and the atmosphere. Many of the shops there shut.

It was too hard for them to remain open with the numbers allowed in per square meter and staff. We went for breakfast at a well known place there. The owner rushed out and offered us a look at the special board. We went in and she was so sad with all her restaurant had been through. Yet with excitement in her eyes, she said "Christmas will save us then the tourist will be back from overseas next year".

As I sit here and write tonight, I think of her and the many that will now be empty at the biggest time of year. New Year's Eve in Sydney.

They shut off the Northern Beaches on the north side over Christmas, they made from the Blue Mountains to the Central Coast a big circle —we were told not to leave or enter unless we really had too. This kept many families apart over Christmas. Sadly, it affected mine. Rules are rules in Covid-19, none add up to me.

So New Year's Eve tomorrow night sadly all those spots so many gather to bring in the New Year are fenced off. Those living in the circle are allowed only five people per house. A group of ten can gather outside. As they say this will be the super spreader if they do not enforce these rules.

Here in Newcastle, we are allowed to go out to clubs and pubs. There will be bands at some, yet no dancing, no singing and get this... no talking loud. I think I'll stay home this one.

Again, I say nothing but wow. Here if you are at a club and play pokies you must be seated together. When at the casino one had to stand. No drinking at the machines only the bar.

Maybe I'll bring this one in meditating for this world to heal and go back to what we never took for granted this time last year as we danced and screamed happy 2020!

I pray we don't get locked down again and I pray the rest of the world gets to our numbers. They are working and trialling vaccines now. We don't know the long term effects so another thing I pray is they don't make them compulsory. This is just my view of how I feel for now.

CHAPTER 24

Meeting Amanda Jane

After Sheb's workshop I had missed out on a fair I really wanted to be a part of. 'Live Your Light' mind body and soul. I had heard so much about this beautiful soul and so wanted to meet her. I sent the application in and was accepted. She had actually sat and read at a table behind me before this fair.

I had a really bad morning and still don't know how I made it to this fair. I know she was meant to be behind me now and holding me up without either of us knowing. It was a really hard fair, the readers were a bit confined and the energy seemed so thick. My readings that day were all very heavy. So much so I actually asked to be taken down for the last three spots after a reading that took all I had in me.

So, I only got to say a quick hello this day to the angel with the big smile and heart behind me. Before her fair I messaged to say I was on a high over doing my first motivational presentation. I did not know why, I just wanted to share my excitement with her. Well, I found out why. She asked me to do this at her fair. "Oh, wow!", I said "of course". I was full of that old 'you can't', and those voices of fear that stopped me for too long in my life.

Not this time... I pushed through again. The day was here and yes, I was full of fear, I can't lie. The morning was magic, I was booked solid, I was so full of magic that day I felt I was going to burst. I took the reading before stage, off to ground and get ready.

I entered the room and the stage was lit like a fairy garden, and I froze—it looked huge to me and I lost it. A good friend had a stall by the stage, I turned to her near tears and said "I can't do this". She smothered me in calming oils.

I looked down and I had my red shoes on. There's some magic in those red shoes... enough to give me the power to take the steps onto the stage. I still remember every single step I took. I looked out at all the faces and I froze. The only thing I could feel was my knees shaking so bad. I actually though I was going to pass out.

The next I knew I opened my mouth and started to tell my life story. I went deep, it was like I was handing what I had locked away for so long, out to anyone it could help. Yet it was about letting it go for me. As I looked around, many were in tears. I thought–oh no what have I done? ...they're all upset. Then the magic took over and my story of healing and finding my key and setting myself free flowed out of me.

Still shaking and with sweat pouring down my body I walked down to Amanda. Her smile and her words were such a relief. She said "wow you just handed it all over and you will be sharing at many more of my fairs".

As I went to leave the room so many people came up to me and hugged me and asked for my work cards. I had touched on so many of their hearts.

I really felt I had failed up there, instead it was my wings opening to fly at last.

This was also the start of a beautiful friendship set up just as we needed each other. The last year was so testing for us both, yet spirit guided us and gave us the information from above from our loved ones to hang in there.

I would get so many messages from her beautiful grandmother June. It turns out June loves to guide me and helps me every day when I'm working in spirit. I think she is trying to make a lady out of me. I must say I have stopped throwing so many naughty words around and I often feel the need to slow down for the client.

When I'm in Spirit I talk so fast. I can't control this or maybe going into another accent. When I've been to fairs that half hour I'm being read seems to fly. So, when I work, I warn of triggers and I take off to give all I possibly can in the time you sit with me. I ask if there is anything you need answers to before we start as I don't want you sitting there thinking, is she going to pick this up? Many say just go with the reading and we always find these questions, and answer them. If not, you again have the chance to ask.

Amanda has asked me to be a part of a beautiful three-day retreat. Something I had on my to do list this year anyway. She had said to me in many readings for me, that I was going to a retreat. Little did we know it was hers.

I sometimes feel so sorry for myself and look back and embrace the poor me. I then look at what she has overcome in her life, and in the last year, and kick my butt and put my red shoes on and dance.

It's the dark days that shows us the light we had already. I myself have learned to embrace the magic in every day now. The little things we take for granted. I see things so much better now. Sadly, we have hard days working in Spirit. Like a nurse or a doctor, we need to hand it over at times.

In our work we can't share who or what we speak of in our healings. It's just like an oath we have. Yet to have her there some days just to understand the energy we use. The pain we feel after a deep reading is a huge blessing. We just get it, I guess. I try hard not to share my personal hard days with many now.

I know if I need her or many of my beautiful circle though, they will be there. In our work it's hard to hide when we are really struggling, though I must say as they all seem to hunt me down and, in the end, I give in and share as they know anyway.

We teach each other from our daily lessons and we all have each other's back.

I found out this week an operation I have to have that will put me out of action for six weeks will now not be till after her retreat. I knew I had to be at this retreat as not only do I get to share my magic. I also get to finish my spiritual healing before my physical one.

CHAPTER 25

Dedication to our beautiful Clair

Last week I woke to the news we had lost one of our beautiful spirit family. Our beautiful earth angel had used her hidden wings to fly over the rainbow bridge way to soon. I had the pleasure of meeting Clair in class when I decided it was time to step into my gift.

Her energy seemed to enter the room and light it up. Her smile and her laugh I will never forget. She was so full of love of Spirit. It was contagious. I quickly learned to sit next to her when possible as Spirit just bounced around her.

She just could not get enough, bless her. I would say we were the naughty girls in the corner. We were just busting to share our gifts. One day in class we all had a turn at picking up any energy in the room.

I got this very funny old soul called Harold. With her huge smile she put up her hand and said he's mine. I had shared much about him that did not add up to me. To her I had brought him back to life.

He was her boss at an Ugg boot factory. So, the glue and all I picked up with fluff made sense to her. With joy she sat and told us all about the jokes they would play on him and him on them. She was so proud to see me get what was to be my first validation. A magic feeling, I will never forget. A magic smile I will never forget.

I had just finished my physic mediumship course so I went out that Friday night to celebrate with a few too many drinks. Sitting with the club social organiser, full of courage I asked if I could do a physic fair there.

She accepted to my shock and after I woke the next day and had that, what did I do last night feel I remembered I was running a fair. Thinking was this spirit or too much spirit I thought okay let's do this.

Clair was the first person I asked and of course she accepted with so much excitement. I was very stressed on the day as I feel I had taken on too much. I had a lot of stall holders downstairs and four readers and Lou doing Reiki upstairs.

In hindsight I should have not read myself or had someone running the show. The bar staff had the bookings list and we sold out. My stress levels were high as I looked over at Clair setting up her table. She was so in her element. Smiling and kissing her cards and blessing them.

This made my heart sing. I went over to her and she smiled that beautiful smile and said calm down sweetheart it will all be just fine. She just did not know stress she just lived in the moment bless her. Her energy actually calmed me down and the day was magic.

Anything with her there was magic I quickly learned. She had a love of chakra healing as strong, if not stronger, than mine. She had a chakra balance bed she loved like her baby. I would see her at many fairs with it, sharing her pure magic and love with many she blessed.

One day I asked her if she would like to run meditation through Shazell. She had learned to use this gift she had as well. Her voice was so soothing. She would arrive and set up the space to work her magic.

This was a very quiet humble Clair I had not seen. Not only did she guide us with meditation she would teach us to only bring a positive intention into the room. To sit in silence and let the energy just flow.

It was hard for me as I was used to being the one in charge in Shazell but she sure did stop me and take control. We all closed our eyes and her voice would guide us to another place. It would flow so beautiful.

I opened my eyes once and she was so angelic sitting cross legged on my bed just rocking side to side and letting it flow through her to us through her words of peace. I would look forward to every Tuesday.

As we would leave some of the girls would come and ask me questions or talk. Well, I do love a good chat. She would say. "please all leave Ellen and go home in the energy we just brought into our souls".

These sessions took place for a long period of time and we all loved these beautiful times with her.

This quiet little soul seemed to come out of her shell and keep growing in her opinions of the world. It was like Covid-19 woke a sleeping giant in her. She was never one to hold back in her view on things. She defiantly was not scared of letting us all know what she felt of the whole situation. I must say I looked forward to her jokes and post every day on Facebook.

She would travel and go out and have so much fun, it was like it flowed from her soul. Yet it was like she had a message she wanted us to know before she left and let's say she pumped it out to us for sure. So many would bite and fight her, yet she did not back down and held her own. She did not fight she just kept saying it as she saw it.

The funny thing here was it's how so many of us see it. She knew and she was never be one to be boxed in our girl. For this I am so proud of you honey.

She came for a reading share with me one week. She was so excited she had left a relationship and true gypsy style, she packed up her house and brought a beautiful little van she called home for the rest of her life.

I will never forget her joy as she took me for what she called a tour of her new home. It was so her and she was so happy. My favourite saying is I would live in a tent if it was full of love. Well, this van sure was full of love and magic.

She lost her father and finally brought Omni Dreaming to life in a shop. She was so excited for me to come over and do a healing read and share there. Today I feel so bad that my busy life did not get there.

If there is one huge lesson, I learned losing her, is never put off those catch-up dates with friend as it may be too late. She worked and travelled in her van and shone her love and light to so many that needed her.

When we had drought and fire in NSW she got in her van and headed out to help in every way she could. To her it was just what she did without a second thought. She went into many houses and places where family had lost members as they just could not go on.

She helped all she could and returned from time to time to see her family and friends.

She started doing lives from her van. I sit and laugh as I write this as she did not seem to like technology. Also, technology plays up with spirit, this I know from watching so many of us on our live readings.

She would set it up and move her head around to fit in the screen, she would laugh her head off. Her trusted cards all set out I front of her. I love to watch her shuffle the cards and wow could she lay a spread out so quick in the perfect arch.

I still have cards flying everywhere trying to do this. Maybe you could lend me a Spirit hand Clair??

It was only the other month I jumped on one of her lives and asked if she could see if my book would be a success. She had a beautiful friend who would sit and read the questions to her and the magic would just flow.

I was on holidays and put phone down to do something, I jumped back on and asked again. She said "Ellen we just read about a book for you". I said "no that was not me". She laughed and said, "well there must be two Ellen's writing a book". True Ellen style I said "oh okay, wow that's cool".

I blame Spirit for my mind at times, although it's the opposite, when I am in Spirit it all just flows and I find so many answers. Clair sure did–her readings were so beautiful to watch and listen to. I would be captured by her hands. She really was a magician with Spirit.

I saved her last live as she was reading a client very close to me and I wanted to go back and watch it all when I found time. Little did I know her time with us was to end only a few days later. This will always be special to keep and go back and watch her in her favourite place… working with Spirit.

Blessings from her heart—it was never about the money for her. A true earth angel gone too soon. This lifetime has for her has ended. It has been a huge shock for all of us that loved her, yet a huge honour to be blessed by all she gave selflessly.

Clair your smile will live on in my heart.

I thank the universe and God every day for blessing me with crossing paths in this journey we call life. I will not say rest in peace, as rest is not a word you seem to know. So, to you my sweet new angel peace be and bless be, darling girl.

CHAPTER 26

Finding your Key to Happiness

I felt it was time for me to step it up and step out on my own. My first workshop. Why not put it out there and see how I go? I made the event and put it up hoping to get a little interest.

To my shock as soon as it went up there was a lot of interest. I could not believe it was sold out within two days. My yellow brick road was about to come to life.

The day arrived and I was so excited. No fear, just full of magic that had been going through my head for weeks I was so keen to finally share.

My daughter Cody shocked me by saying she would come and help me with this workshop. She is scared of Spirit and had never seen me work the floor before. There were a few nerves there I must admit—I wanted her to be proud of me. I wanted her to see the fire that burns in my soul to heal others. I wanted her to see Spirit is good and when I worked with it, I can make it fun.

There was also a lot I had not really shared till just before this workshop that would have been hard to listen to about my past. I need to share this at workshops and as you have read in my book so you can all see where I have come from. Also, why it's my heart work to never leave anyone alone and lost. I can get to and share the healer I found within me on this journey to this workshop.

She greeted them all and each one of them loved her by the end of the day. I don't think I could have done this one without my girl there.

It came time to read the room, the Spirit in that room that day was so beautiful. My connections to each and every one of them was magic. So many validations from the other side. Some very hard and emotional. It's so hard to stand strong out there and not cry with them or just hug them and not let them go.

I never walk away till I know they are okay. Spirit is great at giving me something funny to make them smile and remember the happy times. If they don't, I have been known to try to steal shoes or bags to get them laughing.

I go on that roller coaster with them and I like to leave them on a high. Funny, lots like to challenge me out there, game on- I'll play, at this workshop I had struggled with a lady. I went to walk off in defeat when I heard a male voice say ask her this. Let's just say this funny man trumped her big time.

I have to say every time I walk from that floor or stage it's a huge relief as I am out there working so hard. Not to prove I am a physic clairvoyant. To prove they can communicate through me, they are still there watching over us till we meet again. That's where the magic is you see.

I had a friend fighting cancer with all-natural forms of healing. He went to his doctor for a routine check and before he knew it, he was in hospital all alone being told he not only had one stage four cancer, it had metastasised to his pelvic bone as well. He had been coming to me for Reiki but the power of his mind was so strong that cancer was in for a hell of a fight. I've asked him to share his story in my book in more detail.

I am so pleased he is happy to share with you all, as he is all this book represents. He found his healer within.

I asked him to share on the day and was not sure if he would. As I said, he held a key here to show the power we hold within us.

Well, he shared and he shared, it was like as he shared, he was not only teaching he was healing himself. It was all flowing out of him all his emotions all his fears, but most of all his determination to beat this.

I was giving him signals it was time to wrap it up, he was flowing and in a world of his own, he added so much humour he had the room laughing and crying all at once. I did not want to stop him yet I think he would still be up there if I did not end up going up and dancing him over to his chair next to his beautiful wife.

Time had flown we had been there three hours and I had another speaker to share her story. We took a lunch break. In this time, I like to get around and meet everyone. By now they have all come out of there shell and want to share with me.

I was so blessed by Cody and Rose who helped me so much to set all the food out and clean it all up for me, this gave me more time to talk with people, yet half an hour is not enough and my learning on this day was to have a longer break next workshop.

Everything in life is a learning lesson for sure.

The afternoon started and I was in my magic. I can't explain it, my greatest wish is to heal others. At these events I just want to flow and teach people how to grow like I have. Now we all know I love to talk, yet get me up there and I can freeze up.

I trust in spirit and all my angels and it just seems to flow out of me like magic. So, at the beginning of the day, I had asked how much would they all pay for their key to happiness. Most said huge amounts of money.

Yet no amount of money could buy this key as we know.

I asked them all if they had a super power, what would that be. Instead of to fly, to be invisible, to be magic even their answers were so beautiful and selfless.

To heal the world, to build animal shelters, to help homeless people. I was impressed. My answer was simple. I have my super power—to heal others with my heart and soul.

I feel sometimes it's so unfair to see and hear so many heart-breaking stories Yet again here they all come to learn how to grow from there life paths, but more important, to share how they found the strength to grow and rise as they heal.

I wish these days could last longer as they just seem to be coming out of their shell and time runs out. I asked if anyone would like to share their story or what they got from the day. It's funny... they all froze on me.

Yet it was obvious the energy in the room had shifted so much. I like to end the day with a guided meditation. This one was a beautiful shamanic one on finding your spirit guide. It was raining outside and all the girls had already found a nice place to snuggle up. I looked around the room and had to pinch myself that I was here running this magic day. The time had flown so fast, I had one beautiful job left to bless them with. As they all stayed in the energy of their meditation, I moved around the room giving them all Reiki.

My heart and hands felt like they were on fire. I worked my way around the room on my hands and knees to bless them all with a part of my soul. When I share Reiki, my aim is to connect my soul with their soul and let them fly.

Just like that I looked at Cody smiling at me from the kitchen and it was done. My first workshop was complete. I must say I was so tired with all the energy—it was all like a big blur. I did not know if I had done a good job or not.

Next thing arms and hugs came running at me, they loved it and were already asking when the next one was. I had finally believed in myself enough to step out of my comfort zone and own all my gifts and put them on show.

I can't thank Cody enough for one, just being there to support me and finally see me in action, and also for all her help with making sure every person there did not go without a thing. Also, my beautiful Rose—she has never missed me on stage from my first platform. Her smile grounds me each time. A true earth angel.

I don't think I'll ever forget the feeling I felt driving home that night with Cody.

Magic, pure unadulterated magic.

CHAPTER 27

Set Yourself Free

I was so shocked to be asked so much over the next few weeks, when the next workshop would be. I thought no way will I get many again so soon. Well, I was wrong. I left it about six weeks and thought I would make a new event to see if I got any interest. To my shock I got so much I decided to go ahead with another day of magic. I asked a few guest speakers again to share their stories of healing.

I wanted to change this one up a little but could not think how. A trip to the Bay with my girls gave me the answer I needed. We stopped off to see Lou and went to my favourite little café. Lemon Tree Café–a cosy little, dog-friendly place to meet up. The owner Julie took some time off to sit and talk Spirit with me.

We got to chatting about her love for belly dancing and 'bam' there it was. I wanted them to set themselves free and jump out of there comfort zone. As we drove to the motel the idea hit me and I could not wait to ask her.

She accepted with joy and so much excitement. Little did I know she was actually scared stiff, bless her.

I had asked another two ladies to share their story on the day but it seems like this one was to be all about my magic.

I had made this one an hour longer as I wanted to spend more time one on one over the lunch break. We had so much time to fill—so I was thinking.

Everyone arrived and the excitement in the room was electric. I still cannot believe they're all there to see me. They all find their comfy place–as I like them to be laid back–especially as it had been such a long day.

There are a few smiling faces from my last workshop so I am careful not to repeat too much of the last one. My nerves hit and I fight to rise above them, spirit must take over because I can feel myself talking, see them all smiling then I just seem to get lost in the flow.

I opened up with my story of what was not an easy life. It brings lots of tears but I have to be open to show them where I have come from and that instead of living the "poor me "life as I was. I decided to rise and try to heal others who had the same past as me.

There are so many things I went through that I resonate with—many of the things these people have been a victim of like me. I want them to be a survivor like me as well.

I stood there and guided them through my broken yellow brick road as I call it. The past can't be changed, yet it can be healed. I feel I can put my broken bricks back in place now you see.

As I stood there, I heard myself say do I forgive who stole my childhood. No, I can't yet. Do I thank them. Yes, as they made me a fighter and I'll never give up my fight and my fight to help others to find their key to set them free and grow from anything holding them back.

There I was chatting away and the clock was ticking so fast.

So, we rode the roller coaster and I shared my way of dealing with the past. I have a beautiful chest I use. The one closest to me is silver, in that chest I held so many unanswered questioned I had been asking so many years of my life.

I could not heal till I found the answers here. As much as I tried, I just kept having flashes and trying to put this puzzle together. I would shut it–yet not long after this I would open it as I was not at peace with my past.

When the world shut with Covid-19 it all hit and became so clear. With the help of a councillor, we found the answers.

On another trip away with my daughter beside me, I received a text that finally confirmed I was correct in all I looked for all those years. The shock hit and the tears flowed. A strange feeling of freedom came over me within those tears that night.

I finally moved this part of my life to my gold chest. You see it has a magic lock I can never open. I don't need to as I don't need to go back there ever again. I don't have to worry if people don't believe me—sadly this happens so often. I am free and those who stole my childhood will not steal the rest of my life.

I looked out into a paddock I had passed many times with my family in my childhood, and in my mind's eye I threw that gold chest into the paddock to stay. I thought that night 'why put this in a paddock?' they don't deserve that.

Then I heard my sister Cathy laugh and I saw her beautiful smile, 'You threw them in cow shit Sis. You won't go back to dig that chest out'.

With all my magic little ways I shared with them, I felt I had covered many small ways I found to heal. I don't like to complicate healing—there are many ways and many formulas, yet to me I like to bring them to life through magic, simple, funny lessons.

I then went into my life blessing—I am a psychic clairvoyant.

I have been as long as I can remember. It's my time to shine, it's my time to own this blessing. Many will go against this gift—we get mocked, we get talked about and called fake. Maybe there are fakes out there.

I am not one of them.

I have told many, all my life, things that are going to happen, things about past loved ones. I am not the sort of person who would lie to someone about something so precious.

Most of my work is with the families left behind after someone takes themselves home. A very touchy, sensitive subject and has to be worked with so gently.

This is why I started to bring my gift to life—never did I think Shazell would grow to make me all I am today. I thank God every day for this gift and I feel I only use it as I am guided.

So once again I stepped into my red shoes and took to the floor. So many validations, so many tears of joy. The energy in the room that day was on fire. It's not easy with a room full of Spirit for thirty people to figure out who owns the messages.

Yet with the help from my guides, we find them and we deliver.

It felt like I had been walking the floor for five minutes. I looked at my watch and I was close to two hours. Oops!... I do get lost when I drop into Spirit.

We took an hour for lunch to recharge. I was really feeling this workshop—as I had been in spirit so long—so, we came back from lunch all full of sugary energy from the cakes and treats. It was time to dance.

I had lost Julie and was thinking 'oh no my belly dancer has done a runner on me'. Next thing bells and scarves came dancing through the door. The whole place jumped to their feet and started to go with the flow.

It was so much fun, they jumped out of their comfort zone

and set themselves free. Julie owned that floor and boy can this lady dance. She had done what I wanted to see—she had got them all up. She had not only done that she'd also beaten her own anxiety.

Never dull your shine Julie—you are magic woman–you rock.

The afternoon was coming to an end and I had picked a beautiful meditation to share with them to start the wind down. I told them all to get comfy and turned the music on. I tried and I tried but it wouldn't play. Okay... stay calm Ellen and play another one. No this was just not happening. So, to set myself free from fear I did what I had to do.

I lead them on a guided meditation. It was just flowing from me and we went on a beautiful journey setting ourselves free while healing our chakras. When I ended and looked around the room, they all looked so different to when they had arrived in the morning.

There was one job left for me and this was a Reiki share. I had not had enough water and I was so running out of magic. I tried my music and to no surprise... it worked. The first couple I shared with one of them was opened up so much she was in tears. Her partner beside her started coughing and could not stop.

Reiki is love and cannot hurt—a few months after this workshop we were shown why this has happened to them both.

I crawled around the floor that day to be on their level and shared all I had in me. I looked at Rose that day as I did not think I could finish this one. I could see her concern, yet it was like she shared her energy to get me to the finish line again.

I did it. I was so happy as I got so many hugs and went on just enough of a high to get me home. Rose, I could not have done this one without you my beautiful friend.
That night so many messages of congratulations came through. I was finally so proud of Ellen Louise.

CHAPTER 30

Rebirth at the Waterfalls

Sitting here, over a year from when I first started this book, I'm finally ready to write my final chapter. In the beginning I would have never thought it would have taken so long. As I sit here, I see now that it had to. This book has healed me as I shared it with you. My only wish here is that it helps heal even a small part of you.

It had to wait till today for me to finish it as a magic trip away chasing waterfalls with my husband as a gift for my fifty ninth year in this lifetime. It ended up being the beginning of a new Ellen for the rest of this life time. I feel I was reborn at those waterfalls.

My day started waking up to a message from a long-time client saying. Ellen, I dreamt I watched you being born again. She said it was so clear she could not believe it and had to share it. Funny I wrote back as this trip is for me to leave all the pain of my past behind and walk into my new life ahead of me.

I walked out to the front of my cabin and sat and listened to nature, the view in front of me was breathtaking. I took it all in. I think I could have sat there all day.

We headed to Dorigo, New South Wales. What a breathtaking drive it was out in the beautiful country we are blessed to live in. The smell out there just soothes my soul. It's so lush and green–a far cry from this time a year ago when we were in drought and many farmers lost their farms.

We headed around the winding mountain to the Dangar Falls. As we pulled up I could hear the sound of the water flowing so free and pounding into the dam below it. I lose myself in this moment and nothing can stop me from getting to the waterfall.

Not even a gate that said—falls are closed—we climbed over the gate and not far along the path there she was—so majestic with the sun shining over her crown. We climbed down the mountain side to the base. I could and maybe needed to stand there for hours.

I stepped down into the water and did my waterfall wash off mantra. I wanted to swim out to them as many do but I was told to take a float to rest as they're hard to get to with the power smashing into the bottom. I asked Greg to swim out with me and even he was not keen as it was a very cold day for February and the water was like ice.

I slid my way up the mountain to the car, I was upset with myself as I so wanted to dive into my new life that day through that waterfall—it wasn't meant to be this day and found out later why.

We stopped off for the best pie I have eaten in my life at the bakery in Bellingen—what a cute little town, the baker walked out and I was telling him I've travelled the world and never eaten a pie like this one. We had finished and I wanted to go take a picture in front of the wall art across the road.

He was heading to his car for a lunch break and I'm sure he thought I was chasing him to get his recipe–I had to laugh. I think one day in my future we will move to a place like this on a property and get lots of animals and maybe learn it's okay to do nothing some days.

As we were heading back to our little cabin I looked onto a paddock and I saw a cow laying in a very strange position. She was a golden colour cow—so beautiful. As I looked closer, I could see she was giving birth to a calf.

I made Greg turn around and drive back to her. I jumped out into the long grass with no fear of snakes—I needed to help her. As I went to run across the busy road, Greg stopped me. He said "Ellen what do you think you're going to do?". "Why help her give birth" I thought and spoke.

He of course talked some sense into me thank god, as the other cows were coming quick to protect her. I was trying to find a number of the farm owner to ring them as I was so worried for her. We watched her for a while and she was only in early stages, I wanted to stay and watch this amazing gift of birth and make sure she was okay. I sent all the love and light I had in me and prayed for safe arrival earth side for this little calf.

As we drove home, I calmed down and took in all the county side. Then the words rebirth popped back into my mind. Wow had I just actually witnessed this as I was trying to do my own rebirth.

Spirit sure has a way of showing me things and this seemed to all add up so clear. As we got home, I got a text from my mother she had to have some very serious tests done. My heart was in my throat—she has won her battle with cancer before and I never want to see her have to go into battle again.

She has a beautiful man who is the closest thing to a father I have ever had—she has been through way too much loss in her life losing my Daddy G and my beautiful sister, also another man she loved with all her heart as well.

I just want her to have peace in her life now, so if she has any scares like this one, I'm her rock. I'll always be there for her and I'm blessed to know her beautiful partner will be standing on the other side of her.

I rang and tried to calm her. I have her in my prayers and I'm sending all the healing I have in me till we get these results.

Some friends in need that night needed me, so I reached out and helped them through their situation. My mind was exhausted—this could not be my rebirth day surely? I finally put my phone down—my work was done and I fell into a deep sleep.

The next morning, I woke to the birds singing and the sun shining. The day before we had been only four minutes drive away from Ebor Falls. A couple had said you must see them when we were at Dangar.

To my surprise Greg said "I'm taking you to Ebor Falls get ready and we will get breakfast on the way". I was so excited I think I was in the car and ready within five minutes.

We stopped at an old butter factory on the way for a divine breakfast and off we headed. As we started to rise to the top half off the mountain my phone went off. I found this funny as there is no reception up there as I tried to share a waterfall photo the day before at the very same spot coming home.

I opened it and it was Carmen my book cover artist. She had many setbacks in trying to bring this cover to life. The way it had all fallen into place is a story of its own. Carmen came to me for a reading. Not long into the reading I asked her why she put her brush down.

She replied, "life had got busy looking after a family member" I replied "yes, I know but when you paint you go into Spirit so this is your escape. You will paint again". As I was writing thinking about the cover for my book. I saw this beautiful bright colour painting with my mind's eye. That night I think I was talking to Carmen's daughter and it hit me. "Oh, my... I need your mother to paint my book cover".

I could not wait to get on Messenger and ask her if she would do this for me. With much excitement on both ends, she agreed. Double magic, I get my book cover, she goes back to a gift that has so much more to be shared.

So back to the mountain, her message said, 'my darling I have immersed myself and your portrait in chakra colours this last week which indicate the current emotional and physical states of a human being, fitting symbolism for your Healer Within book cover. I am happy with the essence of beauty of you I see and feel, I hope you feel it too. A sign of hope and promise'.

I had waited so long to see how she had brought my vision to life. Tapping madly on the screen of my phone it wouldn't load... I had to wait till we were back down the mountain to get reception and so I could see this magical image Carmen had created for me.

I put my phone down and as we got close to the waterfall on the side of the road, I picked it up again to try and catch the beauty of this huge waterfall so close by. There I was staring back at myself. My cover—me with all the colours of the rainbow in and around me.

I burst into tears—it was just perfect. There I was on top of a mountain, next to a waterfall and my book cover finally revealed itself. I was crying—something I never do, I was so overjoyed as I listened to KD Lang sing 'Crying' on the radio.

I wanted to message her back, but my fingers were shaking with excitement, finally I sent back... 'I love it so much I am crying'. I also said as she knows Spirit as well as me.. 'and would you believe KD Lang's song Crying is playing full bore at the top of a mountain right now?.

Her reply was 'oh wow! serendipity'.

We arrived at the falls and I felt like I could fly over the top of them. Standing at the top they were massive, and we were told you can't get to the bottom. You would need to be a mountain goat. I am a Capricorn but climbing down a mountain face with my fear of heights—even for a waterfall—is not my idea of fun.

We had to walk on the side of the mountain on a track to get to the falls, there was no rail, and I was nearly running as I could hear them pounding as loud as thunder—my heart was pounding out of my chest.

The first part of the falls was huge, it took my breath away with its enormity. I stood mesmerised by the magic of nature and the flow of this huge fall. A couple walked by and encouraged us to keep going... the next falls are amazing. Next fall's okay I thought it was just another angle of these ones.

So again, with no fear of falling I ran to the next lookout. I have never seen a waterfall like it. As I looked, I could see statues in it with water falling around them. So many different formations as I looked across from one side to another. I was crying, I was covered in goose bumps and I felt blessed to be there.

I stopped on the way back and took many pictures to share. Every waterfall I have ever seen has had huge faces in the rock—faces watching over them. As I went back past the first fall I looked, and I could see it was then like two sides to the fall.

I took a video to share on Shazell. I saw it like birth, when the water as one, parted into two falls, like birth we become two as we leave the mother's womb. When the water hits the bottom, they join again, and the catchment guides the new water to the flow of the new path that lays ahead.

We drove home and every song that came on was so relevant to the way I felt that day.

I sung all the way home. *'For once in my life'* by Stevie Wonder came on and I thought to myself yes, I do. Me, I had found me and all that I needed to be me, up there.

You see the day before had been such a hard day–it was like the labour to my rebirth. This day when I sat and looked at the sunset over the water—that was my rebirth.

The waterfall was me–Ellen–as I lived to please all around me and hide this beautiful gift.

It was time for spirit Ellen to own her gift. We joined at the bottom, we left the past behind and we became one.

I will not hide my gift anymore; I was blessed and within this blessing I found the healer in me.

I am free. Bless be.

Ellen x

In their own Words

Kellie

When my younger brother took himself home, my life, my family, my world shattered. I felt like I had been thrown spiralling down the darkest abyss, with no way to slow down, with overwhelming thoughts of guilt, shock, and grief, I wanted to give in to the darkness. I felt like I belonged there, that it was a karma I deserved.

The night of my brother's passing, I felt this unbelievable urge to reach out to Ellen. I have to admit, I was sceptical, and had narrow minded thinking. I had never had any experience with anyone who had psychic or mediumship abilities and I did not have hope, however I had nothing to lose. Immediately reaching out to Ellen online, she confirmed the insides and outs of my brother's passing, particulars no one could have known, and also facts we confirmed later.

Ellen was a presence, that night I felt her energy scoop me up, and surround me with love and comfort. It was like speaking to my brother Joel, right when I needed it, there is no price that I could ever pay Ellen that would be enough, and I am forever grateful.

Ellen has continually guided and supported me and even given myself and family sessions and her unlimited time for no charge, even though before that day I was a stranger. Ellen's talents go well beyond her mediumship abilities, her healing is pure magic. Her positive energy, her own personal accomplishments and her continuing uplifting words continue to guide myself and others find their way out of the darkness.

Thank you for your magic Ellen, never stop sparkling.

Amanda Jane

Ellen has a special and rare kind of heart. She is pure love and light. Ellen has provided me with so much guidance and insight spiritually over the years that has not only blown me away but also healed many of wounds, allowing me to move forward with my life with peace.

Ellen has also given me some the most magical and powerful Reiki healings I've ever had in my life. This woman has a special gift and now I'm proud to call her a dear friend of mine.

Jess

What can I say but amazing. This lady has gone above and beyond to help me through some of the toughest times of my life. Her positivity, encouragement, strength and guidance has been nothing short perfect. This lady has shown and taught me how to love myself but most of all helped me find me.
To heal and to let go. Forever an inspiration in my eyes

Deb

I could not have found a person to help my baby bro find his way to the other side until I brought you to meet my brother. I was amazed at the first meeting and healing you done for Deanie so much stress was released from his face. After you left he was talking to me about the reiki and said you are a true master but not as high as him, such a smart arse a times but he was so amazed with you my beautiful caring angel as I call you at.

Jody

Standing on a cliff one day, my thoughts of only wanting to jump, I remember walking down to that cliff and two butterfly's were constantly flying into my face, I had no idea I needed them they were the two things along with Ellen that would save me and restore me to my true path I would never have gone down there. But I sat on that cliff for hours reflecting on all the hurt that had been done to me in this lifetime so far, as time went by, looking out across the water and butterfly's in my eyes. I turned around with my guides and found Ellen.

The day I walked into her door she handed me a piece of paper, on that paper was everything I was meant to be, without ever meeting me, Ellen's sister had guided me to her that day after finding out I was sitting in the same place her beautiful sister had died. I new I was different I had always felt I was different but finally after so many long years I finally felt I had truly found myself and it was okay to be different, for what I had was a healing power to be given in this world. A sharmanic natural healer and I finally understood what it was to be me. To accept me for who I am and it was okay to be uniquely me.

Ellen has been guiding me on my path of life's ups and downs, and is now a person I could truly call a friend. With her magical gifts they led me to my true guide and my tribe. The healer healing the healer is such an amazing journey and I thank ellen for every step she has taken me on and through with my heart in hand and soul flying free. My eyes are wide open of all the wonders if what can be.

Moya

Where do I start? Little did I know on the day I went to have my first reading with you, just who I was soon about to meet and learn I was truly going to be in the presence of one of the most gifted, beautiful, talented souls I have ever met! You my beautiful, precious lady have a heart that holds an abundant and endless amount of love for others, that goes way beyond words. Your devotion in helping others and saving lives is endless and so inspiring! You have this amazing magical ability to give so much of yourself in all that you do! I believe we call souls like you our EARTH ANGELS! Because I know you truly are one!

Your light shines out and touches so many souls everyday, no matter how you're feeling in yourself, which you give so much of..You're such an extraordinary soul that has touched so many lives..I just want you to know how blessed I am just by having you in my life. As well as how much you're loved and adored you are by all who know you! Your always there to light the way for others my gorgeous friend. Your words of comfort, encouragement and inspiration keeps so many of us pushing, encouraging us to continue, to take one step at a time and just by seeing how brave and courageous you are in never giving up on your own dreams and healing in your own journey!

It encourages us all to keep going!

Your loved by so many. I pray you know and realise just how much. You have blessed us all just by being your true Authentic self and that in itself is such a special gift to us all precious lady. I'm so grateful that you were sent to me from the Angels I'm sure of that! Thank you sweetheart for everything you have done for me as well as everyone else's life that you have touched and continue to do so. Love & Light always. Namaste our beautiful Earth Angel!

Donna
I would like to share my journey on how I met beautiful Ellen. I like to refer to Ellen as my "Earth Angel". After my late partner "Cindy Jane Flynn" aka "Flynnie" to me (28th December 1979 - 6th October 2016) grew her wings and made the choice to transition over to the Spirit realm. I was left feeling empty and in a very dark place my world had been shattered. I knew I had to connect and was drawn to beautiful Ellen who was then based in Kahibah. I walked into the shop and there stood my beautiful earth angel with her arms wide open and said "I've been waiting for you". I knew I was safe and felt so much comfort wrapped in her arms. From that day Ellen has been such an inspiration to me as Ellen knows exactly about the devastation the aftermath of suicide leaves on those left behind.

Ellen continued to guide me, heal me with her beautiful friendship with her reiki—her amazing talent to connect to the Spirit world, her workshops, Ellen helped to give my soul peace and has given me reassurance that our loved ones are still with us. With Ellen's knowledge passed onto me I have had so many signs that Flynnie is still with me and that brings much comfort.

Moving forward to my gorgeous 1st Born daughter "Chloe May Mittmann" who suddenly passed on the 18th November 2020 who will "forever be 23". Born on the 20th February 1997. Ellen was there to catch me and guide me as it is still early days and still very raw. From the moment Chloe passed Ellen has been here for me, I have to say with everything that I have learnt from you Ellen I know my daughter Chloe will never leave my side.

You have taught me that our loved ones can still hear u, see us, and feel us and that helps me on this horrible road of grief, I feel I'm not just a client of Ellen's—we have formed a special friendship and I am absolutely honoured to called Ellen my

Earth Angel, one of My Dearest and closest friends. So to you Ellen, I want to thank you with my heart and soul, thank you for being you. I love you always xx

To my spirit angels "Chloe and Flynnie" spread those wings of yours and fly high. I love you both endlessly xx

Choices - Gary

Before I begin I would like to thank all of my helpers, well wishers and supporters. This support is so important.

A person on a journey like mine has to combat much more than just a disease. Hearing the wrong word or phrase can tip you over to a world of doubt, anguish and confusion. Hearing the right words will help keep you on track. Ellen gave me her support and time as she does for lots and lots of people and I thank her very much. She has helped me understand the spiritual world. I am not psychic myself but now I do appreciate and accept what other people like her can experience.

We all have good things and bad things that happen to us. Having a specialist in company with two other doctors tell me that I have incurable and aggressive metastatic cancer is the worst that has ever happened to me. He then told me that if he can just keep me alive for a couple of years then something good might come along. I was already in the John Hunter Hospital for a week with a terrible infection that they had given me while having a biopsy for cancer.

It was a blow so hard that I can barely describe it. A bit like leaving my body and going somewhere else. The specialist suggested that I make an appointment to see him in his private rooms and we could have a chat about it. Looking into his eyes I thought: why would I want to do that? He had nothing to offer and no cure had come along in the last hundred years so it is certainly not going to happen in the next couple of years. No, we have nothing to chat about here. That was the first choice that I made on this journey. I have never seen him again.

I told my family that I was going to leave this hospital as soon as I could and go into self treatment. I knew that I would be a mental mess for a long time unless I took control so I told them that I was going to panic for two days and probably go to some depths of despair that I had never been to before and then I was going to come out fighting and I was going to beat this thing! Well, I went to some deep dark places and when I returned, my kids were there to tell me about the research that they had been doing when I was panicking - what a magnificent support team. The nurses were my heroines! I still choke up when I recall how wonderful they were. My favourite was Maddy and I cannot thank her enough.

I had been researching cancer for decades as a kind of intriguing hobby. I was well aware of the disgusting failure rate that doctors have in most chronic diseases. I was also aware of how the pharmaceutical industry is in control of these diseases and the doctors are under their control. This is not a conspiracy theory, it is simply a fact! Let me be clear here. I have nothing against doctors. I accept that they are simply part of a medical industry, part of a system. I have friends who are doctors and they too often complain about this system.

There are hundreds of natural ways of curing cancer. Most are simple and cheap and they almost never have side effects. Some of the best are illegal. They range from things as simple as a change in diet, eating herbs and plants usually available in most countries through to complicated machines. Finding and procuring these things and then taking them is the easy part. The hard part is making the choice to do this. Why would this be the case?

The worst kind of cancer is cancer in the head! By this I mean in your mind. Before you even get cancer in your body you are pre-conditioned to its devastating effects. You grow up hearing about it and sometimes seeing it destroy your friends or family. This was the case for me. Most people live with this dormant fear of cancer. When you are diagnosed with it then this fear is no longer dormant. It comes alive and it is your worst enemy.

Another form of pre-conditioning is the belief that doctors are the only people who can help you get out of this terrible mess. As children our parents tell us that a doctor will fix anything that you get and it usually is the truth verified by your personal experiences as a child and as an adult. When this is reinforced all of your life and it becomes a belief, unshakeable and a part of your mindset. But it is a terribly distorted and controlling belief.

So when a doctor tells you that you have cancer your mind will instantly remind you that it kills because that is your belief. Then if he tells you that there is no cure… well, now your belief system is starting to crash because he was supposed to be able to fix anything. Then he tells you that you are going to die of this cancer in the near future. You are now upset to the max but you are not confused, not at all. You now fully believe that you are going to die and it has been confirmed by an expert. ou now have cancer in the head and your chances of surviving because of that are worse than ever.

I made a different choice. I chose not to believe that I would die from this. I do not mean that I started to think positive that all would be well. I mean that I installed this as a belief. I built this belief by finding evidence to support it and I reinforce it every day. I did not believe that it would be easy, nor did I believe that there would be no set backs. I only believed that I was not going to die from this disease.

Can you see that my chances of survival took a new direction once I believed this?

I believe that cancer is a failure of the immune system. Your body and mind can cure any disease. Cancer can only survive if your immune system is not strong enough to fight it off. So I made a choice to improve and protect my immune system. My self treatment of diet and supplements, exercise, meditation and right thinking began to work after a few months and I started to feel better than I had for years.

I am now approaching the time when according to the specialist who diagnosed me I would be running out of time. But I am happier, fitter and feel healthier than I did way back then. I have had no pain, no illnesses that we usually have and I am stronger in my beliefs than ever before. The choice is ours.

I . am . Me

Is this really magic, is this really me

All the blessings of my life, God has given me.

I want to live my life now, healing with my gift

So I can show them pathways to live there life in bliss.

To bring back passed loved ones they have lost

To guide them with my magic, for me without a cost.

To me this is my heart work, a gift I'm blessed to see

With special angels watching and guiding them to me.

I finally found the healer, the person I'm to be.

So with this gift I'm blessed with

I finally accepted the other side of me.

I am me, I am free, all I wish is bless they be.

www.ingramcontent.com/pod-product-compliance
Lightning Source LLC
Chambersburg PA
CBHW051436290426
44109CB00016B/1572